Good Housekeeping Cook's Year

Autumn
KITCHEN

Good Housekeeping Cook's Year

Autumn
KITCHEN

DELICIOUS RECIPES AND SEASONAL IDEAS FOR AUTUMN COOKING AND ENTERTAINING

EBURY PRESS
LONDON

First published in 1997

1 3 5 7 9 10 8 6 4 2

First published in the United Kingdom in 1997 by Ebury Press
Random House, 20 Vauxhall Bridge Road, London, SW1V 2SA

Random House Australia (Pty) Limited
20 Alfred Street, Milsons Point, Sydney
New South Wales 2061, Australia

Random House New Zealand Limited
18 Poland Road, Glenfield,
Auckland 10, New Zealand

Random House South Africa (Pty) Limited
Endulini, 5a Jubilee Road,
Parktown, 2193, South Africa

Random House UK Limited Reg. No. 954009

A CIP catalogue record for this book is available from the British Library.

ISBN 0 09 185369 9

Managing Editor: Julia Canning
Design: Sara Kidd

Contributing authors: Jacqueline Clark, Maxine Clark, Joanna Farrow,
Jane Newdick, Louise Pickford, Louise Steel, Caroline Richmond Walker
Contributing editors: Helen Southall, Donna Wood
Additional research and assistance: Hilary Bird, Fiona Hunter, Sara Lewis
Recipe testing: Emma-Lee Gow, Patricia Stone

Special photography: Ken Field, Michelle Garrett, Graham Kirk
Photgraphic styling: Michelle Garrett, Roisin Nield, Helen Payne
Food for photography: Maxine Clark, Jane Newdick, Louise Pickford,
Liz Trigg, Joanna Farrow
Colour illustrations: Madeleine David

Printed and bound in Portugal by Printer Portuguesa, Lisbon

**The material in this book was previously published in
Good Housekeeping Cook's Year**

CONTENTS

COOKERY NOTES

- Both metric and imperial measures are given for the recipes. Follow either metric or imperial throughout as they are not interchangeable.

- All spoon measures are level unless otherwise stated. Sets of measuring spoons are available in metric and imperial for accurate measurements of small quantities.

- Ovens should be preheated to the temperature specified. Grills should be preheated. The cooking times given in the recipes assume that this has been done.

- Where a stage is specified in brackets under freezing, the dish should be frozen at the end of that stage.

- Size 2 eggs should be used except where otherwise specified.

- Use freshly ground black pepper unless otherwise specified.

- Use fresh rather than dried herbs unless dried herbs are suggested in the recipes.

- Stocks should be freshly made if possible. Alternatively, buy ready-made stocks or use good quality stock cubes.

AT-A-GLANCE SYMBOLS

❅   The recipes can be frozen

☉   The recipes can be prepared and cooked in 30 minutes or under.

♡   The recipe is under 350 calories per portion for main courses and under 200 calories for starters, accompaniments and desserts.

Autumn

A S AUTUMN APPROACHES, so orchards and hedgerows yield a glorious abundance of fresh fruit, providing delicious flavours for both sweet and savoury dishes. More hearty vegetables start coming into their own again and the style of cooking takes on a more mellow, warming tone, in tune with the changing weather of the season. Halloween and bonfire night are good excuses for casual gatherings, while the rich, russet hues of the falling leaves offer inspiring ideas for subtle table decorations. The pages that follow provide a superb guide for the autumn kitchen, with seasonal decorating ideas as well as delicious and imaginative recipes using the best that the season has to offer.

This is the golden mellow season of abundance. Now's the time to make the most of the cheap and plentiful fruit and vegetables available by turning to the traditional preserving methods. Delicious -tasting jams, chutneys and relishes (see recipes on pages 72-3) are an excellent way of storing abundant produce and will certainly bring cheer to drab winter days. There are some other age-old preserving skills which are also well worth reviving.

PICKLED FRUIT

Freshly picked fruits steeped in spiced sweet-sour syrups are perfect gifts for the Christmas festivities ahead and are marvellous to serve with cold meats as a change from chutney. Try this easy recipe for pickled pears.

Spiced pears For 900 g (2 lb) firm eating pears, gently cook the peeled, cored and quartered pears in water for 5 minutes, then drain. Pour 450 ml (15 fl oz) cider vinegar into a pan with 300 ml (10 fl oz) water, 450 g (1 lb) sugar, 1 cinnamon stick, 10 cloves and a small piece of root ginger. Heat gently, stirring, until the sugar has dissolved then boil for 5 minutes. Add the pears and cook until tender. Remove the pears and pack into sterilized jars. Pour the strained syrup over, then cover immedi-

Crisp and full of flavour, English apples are one of the great pleasures of autumn.

ately with airtight and vinegar-proof tops.

Plums, nectarines and peaches can be bottled in this way too.

PICKLED VEGETABLES

Crisp vegetables pickled in a clear, spiced vinegar are another autumn must. Pickled onions are a favourite.

Pickled onions Place 1.8 kg (4 lb) unskinned pickling onions in a large bowl. Dissolve 225 g (8 oz) salt in 2.3 litre (4 pints) water, pour over the onions and leave for 12 hours. Drain and skin the onions, then recover with the same amount of fresh brine. Leave for 24-36 hours. Meanwhile, make spiced vinegar. Add 25-50 g (1-2 oz) pickling spice to 1.1 litres (2 pints) distilled malt vinegar, bring to the boil, then infuse for 2 hours. Strain through muslin and cool. Drain the onions and rinse well, then pack into sterilized jars. Cover with the spiced vinegar. Top with vinegar-proof tops and leave for 3 months before using.

FRUIT LIQUEURS

Liqueurs made by infusing fruits in spirits for several months are surprisingly easy to make and are a wonderful way of using up ripe autumnal fruit. Damsons in particular can be turned into a warming drink for encroaching winter days.

Damson gin or vodka Using a needle stuck into a cork, prick 900 g (2 lb) damsons all over. Place in a large jar, pour over two 75 cl bottles gin or vodka and add 350 g (12 oz) granulated sugar. Close tightly and keep in a cool dark place for 2-3 months, gently shaking the jar from time to time. Strain and decant into clean bottles.

For an attractive and unusual gift, fill small clean sherry bottles with the liqueur, replace the corks or stoppers and dip the entire top of the bottle in melted sealing wax.

ORCHARD HARVEST

Orchard fruits are abundant at this time of year and can be used in all sorts of sweet and savoury dishes. Apples, pears and plums are particularly useful turned into purées – simply poach the fruit in a little water and sugar, then mash, blend or sieve as necessary.

• To ring the changes, combine apple and pear purée or plum and apple purée. Use as fillings for tarts or puff pastry turnovers. Or mix with thick double cream to make a luscious cake filling.

• Serve spiced purées with roast meats such as pork or duck, or stir a couple of spoonfuls into mashed

root vegetables, such as celeriac or turnip for interesting complementary flavours.

Preserve-making is a satisfying way of capturing the delicious flavours of autumnal fruit and vegetables.

Quick Fruit Ideas

• For an attractive side dish to serve with roast chicken or game, core small dessert apples and fill with a mixture of sautéed bacon and onion, creamy goats' cheese and a scattering of toasted pine nuts. Cook at 200°C (400°F) mark 6 for 20-25 minutes.

• To make a quick, tasty supper dish, brown pork loin chops in a little oil, then wrap in foil parcels with slices of red apple, chopped prunes, chopped herbs, a little apple juice and seasoning. Bake at 180 °C (350°F) mark 4 for 1 hour until tender.

• For an easy dinner party dessert, poach apple rings in a little red wine and cinnamon until tender, sweeten to taste with honey and sprinkle with toasted almonds. Serve with crème fraîche.

• Poach plums in fragrant Earl Grey tea to round off a meal.

• Try adding half a grated apple to a blue cheese and bacon flan.

GAME BIRDS

Game birds are well worth trying as they are almost fat free and provide filling meals. Butcher's game will have been hung to give a full flavour; supermarket game will not have been hung for so long, resulting in a milder flavour. A wide variety of fresh and frozen game is now available from supermarkets. Birds such as partridge, wild duck, pigeon and pheasant can be plainly roasted, or you can simply remove the breast meat and pan-fry or grill it like chicken. Keep it slightly rare to ensure that it remains tender and juicy. Use the remaining carcasses to make rich stock or freeze raw to use later.

Venison is a good lean alternative to beef and can be substituted in any beef recipe. It gives a particular richness to a steak pie if you use half venison and half beef. The secret is to slowly casserole the tougher cuts so that they become meltingly soft.

More tender cuts can be quickly pan-fried with seasonal fruit to make a quick, flavourful meal. Butcher's venison is stronger, so it is wise to marinate it first in wine and vinegar. Discard the marinade and use fresh wine in the finished dish.

All game is good with a sharp fruit sauce as it cuts through the richness - venison with blueberries makes an easy dinner party dish with a difference (see page 34). For a classic way to serve a whole roast bird, quickly sauté the livers in butter, then spread on a fried bread croûte. Place the bird on top – the croûte absorbs the juices from the bird giving it a delicious flavour.

Game chips are a traditional accompaniment. To prepare, peel and cut potatoes into very thin slices, then deep-fry until golden.

Bread sauce is another classic partner to game, and is so easy to make. Stick a few cloves into a peeled onion and place in a pan with a bay leaf and 450 ml (15 fl oz) milk. Bring slowly to the boil, remove from the heat, cover and leave for 10 minutes to infuse. Remove the onion and add 75g (3 oz) fresh breadcrumbs. Season, cover and simmer gently for 10-15 minutes, stirring occasionally. Stir in 15 g (½ oz) butter and 30 ml (2 tbsp) single cream to finish.

ABUNDANT SHELLFISH

With the 'R' returning to the names of the month, this is a very good time for all shellfish, including oysters, mussels and scallops.

For informal, easy entertaining, a 'mussel feast' is hard to beat. Get your friends to help with the scrubbing of the mussels, then cook huge pots of Moules Marinière – for a simple version for 4-6, heat 50 g (2 oz) butter in a large stock pot. Add 2 chopped onions, 3 chopped shallots and 2 chopped garlic cloves and sauté for about 10 minutes until soft. Add 300 ml (10 fl oz) dry white wine and some fresh parsley stalks and bring to the boil. Add 2.6 kg (6 lb) cleaned mussels, cover and boil rapidly, shaking occasionally, for about 5 minutes or until the mussels have opened. Serve with the broth (discarding any unopened mussels). Accompany with lots of French bread and butter.

If you're feeling extravagant, start the feast with half a dozen fresh oysters for each person. Serve with a squeeze of lemon and black bread. Your fishmonger will open them for you, but eat them as soon as you get home to appreciate their fresh sea flavour.

White fish is also excellent at this time of the year, inspiring you to make sumptuous fish pies. A really good fish pie, made up in individual portions, can make excellent dinner party food. Try a combination of jumbo prawns, chunks of flaky white cod and even some smoked fish and sautéed leeks, enrobed in a creamy wine sauce and topped with the fluffiest potato mixed with a little Parmesan and saffron.

HALLOWEEN NIGHT

On the 31st October it's fun to throw a Halloween party, particularly for children who thoroughly enjoy the spooky atmosphere of Halloween night.

Pumpkins

Pumpkins are widely available at this time of year and no Halloween party is complete without a pumpkin lantern. To make a lantern, simply scoop out the flesh, carve a face in the skin and place a candle inside the shell. Don't discard the scooped-out flesh as this can be used to make warming party fare from hearty soup to the all-American pumpkin pie. Puréed pumpkin is particularly good mixed into a baked potato, while slices of pumpkin can be turned into tasty fritters (see page 59).

• To make pumpkin pie, steam 450 g (1 lb) pumpkin pieces between two plates over a pan of boiling water for 15-20 minutes, then drain and purée. Beat together 2 eggs and 125 g (4 oz) sugar, then stir into the pumpkin purée with 60 ml (4 tbsp) milk, 10 ml (2 tsp) ground cinnamon and a pinch each of grated nutmeg and ground ginger. Pour into a 20 cm (8 inch) flan tin lined with shortcrust pastry and bake at 220°C (425°F) mark 7 for 15 minutes, then reduce the oven temperature to 180°C (350°F) mark 4 and bake for a further 30 minutes or until set. Serve warm with cream.

Bewitching Food

Here are just a few more ideas for a Halloween get-together.

• Halve a butternut squash, remove the seeds, pour 30 ml (2 tbsp) maple syrup into the hollow and bake in the oven at 220°C (425°F) mark 7 for 25 minutes. The syrup caramelizes and tastes superb.

• Toffee apples are a must for children. To make the toffee coating for 6-8 apples, heat in a heavy-based saucepan 450 g (1 lb) demerara sugar, 50 g (2 oz) butter or margarine, 10 ml (2 tsp) vinegar, 150 ml (5 fl oz) water and 15 ml (1 tbsp) golden syrup until the sugar has dissolved. Bring to the boil, then brush the inside of the pan with water just above the level of the sugar syrup. Boil rapidly for 5 minutes until the temperature reaches 143°C

(290° F) or when a little syrup dropped into cold water separates into hard but not brittle threads. Push sticks into the cores of the apples and dip into the toffee, twirling around for a few seconds. Leave to set on waxed paper.

• For an adult version - toffee apple tart - bake a pastry case, arrange chunks of sautéed apple in the base, pour over double cream and drizzle over toffee (see above).

• Make a Halloween cake by covering a favourite sandwich cake with green fondant icing or marzipan and top it with a pile of fondant-moulded creepy-crawlies.

• For 'horror hands' arrange sausages in a baking tray in the shape of a hand. Bake at 220°C (425°F) mark 7 for about 10 minutes until browned. Meanwhile, make pancake batter. Pour the batter into the hot tin around the sausages and bake for about 40 minutes. Serve with plenty of tomato ketchup!

• To make 'bandaged toes', wrap bacon around chipolatas or cocktail sausages and bake in the oven, basting with maple syrup or a little treacle.

• Give children going-home presents of black or

A must for every Halloween party; toffee apples, 'bandaged toes' and pumpkin pie.

dark purple sweets, wrapped in black crêpe or tissue and tied with black and red liquorice laces.

BONFIRE NIGHT

Following on sharply from Halloween comes Guy Fawkes night and fireworks parties. Nowadays it is much simpler to go to a communal display and return home for a warming supper. Soup is essential, and a hearty beef and vegetable stew (see page 39) can be kept gently cooking in the oven while you enjoy the fireworks.

• Hot garlic bread is the perfect accompaniment - cut a large French loaf into thick slices and beat 2 crushed garlic cloves into about 125 g (4 oz) butter. Spread the butter generously between the slices, wrap in foil and bake in a medium oven for about 15 minutes.

• For a simple but irresistible pudding, spread thick slices of sticky gingerbread with cream cheese mixed with preserved ginger and a sliced raw apple.

GILDED NUT STOPPERS

Gilded and glued to corks or stoppers, nuts in their shells add a decorative top-knot to vinaigrette bottles, decanters or bottles of wine or sherry. Choose whole, undamaged nuts, such as Brazils, pecans, walnuts, hazelnuts and almonds. An electric glue gun is quick, clean and simple to use, although you can use any strong adhesive to stick the nuts to the corks.

To gild the nuts here, bronze powder is mixed into a paint medium, following the manufacturer's instructions. For a shiny, bright-gold finish, use gold foil leaf or a gold wax polish that is simply rubbed on to the nut and polished with a soft cloth.

Bear in mind that painted corks should be used for decorative purposes only.

You will need:
Bronze powder
Paint medium
**Assortment of nuts in their
  shells**
Sandpaper
**Electric glue gun or strong
  adhesive**
Corks
Paint brush

1 Mix the bronze powder with a little medium to make a gold-coloured paint.

3 Glue a suitable-shaped nut to an appropriate-sized cork and leave to dry thoroughly.

2 Rub one side of each nut with sandpaper to key the surface before gluing it to the cork.

4 Gild the nut on top of the cork or just paint the cork and leave the nut natural.

DECORATED PUMPKINS AND SQUASHES

In the autumn, there is an abundance of pumpkins and squashes on sale at greengrocers and supermarkets. With their brilliant colours and shapes, they need little in the way of decoration to make an impact at a Halloween or fireworks party. Look at each pumpkin and decide how best to decorate it.

Hunt out large-headed brass nails or upholsterers' gimp tacks in ironmongers and haberdashery departments to push into the pumpkins like gold studs. Gold beads and shiny gold leaves from cake-decorating accessory shops can be fixed to the pumpkin with gold wire.

You will need:
Large or small orange-skinned pumpkins and squashes
Gold cord, string, braid or ribbon
Brass studs, large-headed tacks or nails
Fine, small-headed brass pins to attach braid
Gold paper leaves
Gold florist's wire
Gold beads

• Wrap a criss-cross of gold braid around a small pumpkin, or pin twirls of gold cord over the surface of a large one.

• For the simple studded designs, work out where to place the studs by eye. In more elaborate designs it is best to mark out regular positions with a felt tip pen before inserting the studs.
• String gold paper leaves onto short lengths of wire and push them into the pumpkin or tie them around the top.
• Thread a few beads onto lengths of string and drape them around the top of the pumpkin.
• For an impressive grouping, stack a few pumpkins together, with the larger ones at the base and one or two smaller ones balanced on top.

LEAF PRINTS

You can use dried and pressed newly fallen autumn leaves to print beautiful patterns onto fabric or paper. Choose leaves that have an interesting shape with a clear outline, or compound leaves with several small leaves on a single stem. Leaves with distinct veins, such as rose leaves, work very well.

  Many different paints, such as acrylic, poster or water colours are suitable for printing on paper but for printing on fabrics, special colourfast, washable fabric paints are essential.

You will need:
Autumn leaves
Small pieces of thick card
Corks
Adhesive
Acrylic paint
Paint brush
Paper
Scissors
Ready-made napkins or fabric
  for making napkins
Absorbent cloth
Fabric paint

1 Press leaves flat and dry, then glue them onto small pieces of stiff card.

3 Brush a mounted leaf with acrylic paint. Press onto a scrap of paper to remove excess paint, then print. Cut around prints to make labels.

2 Glue a cork to the back of each leaf block to make it easier to hold.

4 For printing on fabric napkins, lay napkin out flat on soft, absorbent cloth. Print using special fabric paint.

FRUIT AND LEAVES BASKET

A glowing arrangement of richly coloured fruits nestling on a bed of dried bracken and fallen leaves in a basket captures all the glorious shades of autumn magnificiently. Positioned on a dresser or sideboard, this stunning display will bring a touch of warmth to any kitchen or dining-room setting.

Rosy apples and pears form the basis of this display, interspersed with more exotic fruits such as scarlet cranberries, black grapes and plums, blooming pomegranates, tamarillos and cape gooseberries (physalis). Mix the fruits as you wish.

You will need:
Oval basket
Foil or clingfilm
Crumpled paper, tissue or bubble wrap for packing
Dried bracken and autumn leaves
Red apples and pears
Black grapes
Plums
Cranberries
Tropical fruits, such as pomegranates, tamarillos, cape gooseberries, small pineapple

1 Line the basket with foil or plastic and then fill the base with crumpled paper, tissue or bubble wrap.

2 Cover the lining with a layer of dried bracken, letting some stems spill over the rim of the basket.

3 Pile up layers of the larger fruit, working so that the display can be viewed either from all sides or from the front alone, depending on where the basket is to be positioned.

4 Drop the small fruits in between the large ones, being careful to vary the colours and textures of the fruits. Open out the papery cover of some of the cape gooseberries to expose the orange-coloured fruit within.

5 As a final touch, tuck some dried leaves in among the fruits to fill in any gaps.

BOUILLABAISSE

PREPARATION TIME 25 minutes, plus soaking
COOKING TIME 20-25 minutes
FREEZING Not suitable

SERVES 6

365 CALS/SERVING

- *900 g (2 lb) mixed fish and shellfish, such as monkfish, red mullet, John Dory, bass, prawns, cleaned*
- *few saffron strands*
- *150 ml (5 fl oz) olive oil*
- *2–3 onions, peeled and sliced*
- *1 celery stick, chopped*
- *225 g (8 oz) tomatoes, skinned and sliced*

- *2 garlic cloves, peeled and crushed*
- *1 bay leaf*
- *2.5 ml (½ tsp) dried thyme or fennel*
- *a few parsley sprigs*
- *finely shredded rind of ½ orange*
- *salt and pepper*
- *about 1.1 litres (2 pints) fish stock*
- *parsley sprigs, to garnish*

1 Skin and fillet the fish if necessary, then cut into fairly large, thick pieces. Remove the shellfish from their shells.
2 Put the saffron in a small bowl. Pour in 150 ml (5 fl oz) boiling water and leave to soak for 30 minutes.
3 Heat the oil in a large saucepan, add the onions and celery and fry gently for 5 minutes, until beginning to soften. Add the tomatoes to the pan with the garlic, herbs, orange rind and seasoning.
4 Arrange the fish in a layer over the vegetables, pour over the saffron liquid and just enough stock to cover the fish. Bring to the boil and simmer uncovered for about 8 minutes.
5 Add the shellfish and cook for a further 5–8 minutes, until the fish pieces are cooked but still hold their shape. Serve garnished with parsley.

NOTE Choose from the wealth of fish and shellfish available at this time of year to create your own version of this mediterranean-style chunky soup.

PARSNIP AND APPLE SOUP

PREPARATION TIME 15 minutes
COOKING TIME 45 minutes
FREEZING Suitable (stage 3)
♡ ❄

SERVES 6

175 CALS/SERVING

- *25 g (1 oz) butter or margarine*
- *700 g (1½ lb) parsnips, peeled and roughly chopped*
- *1 cooking apple, peeled and roughly chopped*
- *1.1 litres (2 pints) vegetable stock*

- *4 sage leaves or 2.5 ml (½ tsp) dried sage*
- *2 cloves*
- *150 ml (5 fl oz) single cream*
- *salt and pepper*
- *sage leaves or parsley and croûtons, to garnish*

1 Melt the butter in a large saucepan; add the parsnips and apple, cover and cook gently for 10 minutes, stirring occasionally.
2 Pour in the stock, and add the sage and cloves. Bring to the boil, cover, then simmer for 30 minutes or until the parsnips are very soft.
3 Remove the sage leaves and cloves; leave the soup to cool slightly, then purée in a blender or food processor.
4 Return the soup to the saucepan, add the cream and reheat gently. Season with salt and pepper. Serve hot, garnished with the sage or parsley and croûtons.

> *TIP*
> This autumnal soup freezes very well, so make a double quantity to save time. It's useful to freeze the soup in single or double portions in readiness for last-minute suppers. Add the cream when reheating.

GARLIC AND ONION SOUP

PREPARATION TIME 10 minutes
COOKING TIME 50 minutes
FREEZING Suitable (stage 2)

♡ ❄

SERVES 6

- *50 g (2 oz) butter*
- *450 g (1 lb) onions, peeled and thinly sliced*
- *8 large garlic cloves, peeled and thinly sliced*
- *30 ml (2 tbsp) white plain flour*

115 CALS/SERVING

- *2 litres (3½ pints) vegetable or chicken stock*
- *2 egg yolks*
- *15 ml (1 tbsp) red wine vinegar*
- *salt and pepper*

1 Melt the butter in a saucepan; add the onions and garlic and cook until golden.

2 Stir in the flour and cook for 1 minute. Remove from the heat and pour in the stock, then bring to the boil, stirring. Cover and simmer for about 30 minutes.

3 Beat the egg yolks with the vinegar. Mix with a little hot soup, then stir the egg yolks into the rest of the soup. Cook over a gentle heat, stirring until the soup thickens slightly. Do not boil. Season to taste. Serve in individual bowls.

TIP
A roast garlic garnish looks attractive and enhances the flavour of this soup. Leave the skins on three small garlic bulbs. Halve each one. Place on an oiled baking sheet. Roast at 170°C (325°F) mark 3 for about 45 minutes or until they are tender.

CHICKEN LIVER AND PISTACHIO PATE

PREPARATION TIME 20 minutes, plus overnight chilling
COOKING TIME 15 minutes
FREEZING Suitable
❄

SERVES 8-10

- *2 rashers of rindless streaky bacon, finely chopped*
- *about 225 g (8 oz) butter*
- *700 g (1½ lb) chicken livers, chopped*
- *1-2 garlic cloves, peeled and chopped*
- *large pinch of ground allspice*
- *125 g (4 oz) flat mushrooms, finely chopped*
- *1 onion, peeled and finely chopped*
- *200 g (7 oz) low-fat soft cheese*

435-350 CALS/SERVING

- *30 ml (2 tbsp) double cream*
- *40 g (1½ oz) shelled pistachio nuts, roughly chopped*
- *45 ml (3 tbsp) chopped mixed fresh parsley, chives and thyme*
- *salt and pepper*

TO GARNISH

- *parsley or other herb leaves*
- *few shelled pistachio nuts*

1 Place the bacon in a heavy-based frying pan and cook until lightly browned.
2 Add 50 g (2 oz) of the butter to the pan and heat until just melted. Add the livers to the pan with the garlic and allspice, and cook briskly over a high heat until the livers are sealed and browned on the outside but still a little pink (but not bloody) on the inside. Remove the bacon and livers from the pan with a slotted spoon and set aside.
3 Add the mushrooms and onion to the pan and cook gently until the onion is softened. Remove from the heat.
4 Transfer the livers and bacon to a blender or food processor. Add the onion and mushrooms, along with any butter remaining in the pan. Add the soft cheese and cream and work until smooth. Turn into a mixing bowl.
5 Fold the nuts and herbs into the pâté. Season with salt and pepper to taste. Spoon the pâté into small individual dishes and level the tops.
6 Melt the remaining butter in a small saucepan over a very low heat. Slowly pour into a jug, leaving the milky sediment behind. Slowly pour the clarified butter onto the pâtés to cover them completely. Immerse herbs and pistachios in the butter to garnish. Chill overnight to set.

VARIATION To make a milder pâté, increase the cream cheese to 400 g (14 oz).

PEPPERED MACKEREL AND APPLE MOUSSES

PREPARATION TIME 30 minutes, plus chilling
COOKING TIME 13-18 minutes
FREEZING Suitable (stage 3)

❄

SERVES 6

- 15 ml (1 tbsp) vegetable oil
- 1 small onion, peeled and chopped
- 225 g (8 oz) cooking apples, peeled and chopped
- 4 peppered mackerel fillets
- 30 ml (2 tbsp) creamed horseradish
- 75 ml (5 tbsp) mayonnaise

380 CALS/SERVING

- 60 ml (4 tbsp) lemon juice
- 15 ml (1 tbsp) powdered gelatine
- salt and pepper
- 3 red eating apples
- few sprigs of watercress or flat-leaf parsley
- 45 ml (3 tbsp) low-fat natural yogurt

1 Heat the oil in a saucepan, add the onion and cook gently until softened. Add the cooking apples, cover, and cook for 10-15 minutes or until the apple has softened. Leave to cool.
2 Flake the mackerel, and put into a blender or food processor with half the creamed horseradish and 30 ml (2 tbsp) mayonnaise. Blend for a minute. Add the onion and apple, and blend until smooth.
3 Put 15 ml (1 tbsp) lemon juice and 15 ml (1 tbsp) water in a small bowl. Sprinkle the gelatine over it and leave to soak for 5 minutes. Stand the bowl in a pan of simmering water and stir until dissolved, then stir into the mackerel and apple purée. Season with salt and pepper. Spoon the mixture into six greased 150 ml (5 fl oz) ramekin dishes. Chill for 2 hours until set.
4 Core and thinly slice the red apples and toss in 30 ml (2 tbsp) of the lemon juice. Arrange on six plates with the watercress or parsley.
5 Dip the mousses briefly in hot water, then unmould them onto the plates. Grind a little pepper over the top. Mix the yogurt with the remaining horseradish, mayonnaise and lemon juice. Season and serve with the mousses.

WARM SEAFOOD SALAD WITH TOASTED POLENTA

PREPARATION TIME 15 minutes, plus cooling
COOKING TIME 15 minutes
FREEZING Not suitable

SERVES 6

- 75 g (3 oz) polenta
- 150 ml (5 fl oz) salad dressing
- 1 garlic clove, peeled and crushed
- 30 ml (2 tbsp) chopped fresh herbs

285 CALS/SERVING

- 350 g (12 oz) smoked haddock fillet, thinly sliced
- 175 g (6 oz) cooked, peeled prawns

1 Make up the polenta according to packet instructions. Spoon onto a sheet of foil, cool slightly, then press into a rectangle about 1 cm (½ inch) thick. Leave to cool.
2 Whisk together the dressing, garlic and half of the herbs. Place the haddock and prawns in a single layer in a shallow, heatproof dish. Pour the dressing over. Cover and chill.
3 Cut the cooled polenta into 7.5 cm (3 inch) triangles. Grill for about 4 minutes on each side until golden.
4 Grill the fish for 1-2 minutes, basting, until the haddock turns opaque. Serve the polenta with the warm salad. Sprinkle the remaining herbs over.

TIP
Polenta is coarse-grained, yellow cornmeal which is cooked in water to a thick paste. The quick-cook variety is suitable for this recipe. Look for it in supermarkets and Italian delicatessens.

1 Place the bulghur wheat in a large bowl and pour over 300 ml (10 fl oz) boiling water. Leave to soak for 30 minutes until the bulghur has softened, then drain off any excess water.

2 Peel the lemon, being careful to remove all the pith. Cut the flesh into segments, discarding the pips. Finely dice the flesh.

3 Combine the bulghur wheat with the lemon and the next seven ingredients. Cover and chill for 1 hour for the flavours to develop.

4 Remove the salad from the refrigerator and stir in the pine nuts, olives and plenty of seasoning. Serve at once.

GRILLED PEARS WITH STILTON

PREPARATION TIME 10 minutes
COOKING TIME 6-7 minutes
FREEZING Not suitable

SERVES 4

- *8 thick slices cut from a large baguette*
- *1 packet ready-washed watercress, trimmed*
- *2 large ripe pears, peeled, cored and sliced*

350 CALS/SERVING

- *225 g (8 oz) blue Stilton cheese*
- *freshly ground black pepper*

1 Toast the bread on both sides then transfer to a baking sheet that will hold the slices in a close single layer.

2 Cover with the watercress and place the pear slices on top. Slice the cheese and arrange over the pears.

3 Place under a hot grill until the cheese is just beginning to melt. Grind black pepper liberally over the top and serve at once.

VARIATION Substitute another blue cheese, such as Gorgonzola or Bleu d'Auvergne.

BULGHUR WHEAT SALAD WITH DRIED FRUIT AND PINE NUTS

PREPARATION TIME 15 minutes, plus soaking and chilling
FREEZING Not suitable

SERVES 4-6

- *225 g (8 oz) bulghur wheat*
- *1 lemon*
- *1 large onion, peeled and finely chopped*
- *4 ripe tomatoes, skinned and diced*
- *75 g (3 oz) dried fruit, such as figs, apricots and peaches, chopped*
- *60 ml (4 tbsp) chopped fresh coriander*

635–425 CALS/SERVING

- *30 ml (2 tbsp) chopped fresh mint*
- *125 ml (4 fl oz) extra-virgin olive oil*
- *5 ml (1 tsp) clear honey*
- *50 g (2 oz) pine nuts, toasted*
- *50 g (2 oz) pitted black olives*
- *salt and pepper*

TIP

To toast the pine nuts, place the nuts on a baking sheet and toast in the oven at 200°C (400°F) mark 6 for 6-8 minutes until golden.

POTATO PANCAKES WITH SMOKED SALMON

PREPARATION TIME 15 minutes, plus standing
COOKING TIME About 30 minutes
FREEZING Suitable (stage 5)
❄

MAKES 6

- *350 g (12 oz) potatoes, peeled*
- *salt and pepper*
- *45 ml (3 tbsp) milk*
- *2 whole eggs, 2 egg whites*
- *45 ml (3 tbsp) single cream*
- *45 ml (3 tbsp) white plain flour*

340 CALS/SERVING

- *oil for frying*
- *175 g (6 oz) sliced smoked salmon*
- *200 ml (7 fl oz) crème fraîche or soured cream*
- *40 g (1½ oz) jar salmon roe*
- *fresh chives and lemon wedges, to garnish*

1 Cook the potatoes in boiling, salted water for 20 minutes until tender. Drain and mash well.
2 Beat in the milk, whole eggs, cream and flour: season well.
3 Lightly whisk the egg whites and fold into the potato mixture. Cover, then leave in a cool place for about 1 hour.
4 Heat a little oil in a non-stick crêpe pan and spoon in about 75 ml (5 tbsp) of the pancake mixture. Cook for approximately 2-3 minutes, then carefully flip over and cook the underside for a further 2-3 minutes. Cook the remaining pancakes. You should have 6 in total.
5 Keep the pancakes hot in a low oven, layered with greaseproof paper and wrapped in foil.
6 To serve, arrange one pancake on individual plates and top with a slice of smoked salmon, a spoonful of crème fraîche and a little salmon roe. Garnish with fresh chives and lemon wedges.

GOLDEN STUFFED MUSHROOMS

PREPARATION TIME 10 minutes
COOKING TIME About 25 minutes
FREEZING Not suitable
🕐

SERVES 4

- *12 cup mushrooms*
- *about 60 ml (4 tbsp) olive oil*
- *175 g (6 oz) rindless streaky bacon, roughly chopped*
- *1 small onion, peeled and finely chopped*
- *50 g (2 oz) salted cashews, chopped*
- *2 garlic cloves, peeled and crushed*

320 CALS/SERVING

- *75 g (3 oz) fresh white breadcrumbs*
- *45 ml (3 tbsp) chopped fresh parsley*
- *1 egg, beaten*
- *salt and pepper*
- *lemon slices and basil, to garnish*

1 Roughly chop the mushroom stems; rinse and drain the mushroom caps.
2 Heat 30 ml (2 tbsp) oil in a medium-sized frying pan and stir-fry the bacon for 2-3 minutes. Add the onion, mushroom stems, cashews and garlic. Cook for a further 3-4 minutes. Remove from the heat.
3 Stir the breadcrumbs, parsley and beaten egg into the mushroom mixture. Add plenty of pepper but only a little salt. Leave to cool.
4 Place the mushroom caps on an oiled edged baking tray. Fill with the mushroom mixture. Drizzle with oil.
5 Bake at 220°C (425°F) mark 7 for 15-20 minutes or until tender and lightly browned. Serve garnished with lemon slices and basil.

FISHERMAN'S PIE

PREPARATION TIME 10 minutes
COOKING TIME 54 minutes
FREEZING Suitable

❄

SERVES 4   390 CALS/SERVING

- *50 g (2 oz) butter or margarine*
- *1 red pepper, deseeded and thinly sliced*
- *1 green pepper, deseeded and thinly sliced*
- *1 small onion, peeled and sliced*
- *salt and pepper*
- *125 g (4 oz) button mushrooms, halved*
- *500 ml (16 fl oz) tomato juice*
- *575 g (1¼ lb) cod fillet, skinned*
- *450 g (1 lb) potatoes, peeled and very thinly sliced*
- *50 g (2 oz) Edam cheese, grated*

1 Melt 25 g (1 oz) of the butter in a frying pan, add the peppers and onion and fry gently for 10 minutes or until soft but not coloured. Using a slotted spoon, transfer to a 2.4 litre (4 pint) ovenproof dish. Season well with salt and pepper.
2 Add the mushrooms to the juices in the frying pan and cook for 3-4 minutes, stirring frequently, until evenly coloured.
3 Pour the tomato juice evenly over the pepper and onion mixture in the dish.
4 Cut the fish into large cubes. Arrange the cubes on top of the tomato juice, pressing down gently into the juice. Top with the mushrooms. Season again with salt and pepper to taste.
5 Arrange the potato slices on top of the mushrooms. Melt the remaining butter and brush over the potatoes. Bake in the oven at 190°C (375°F) mark 5 for 25 minutes.
6 Sprinkle the grated cheese over the pie, return to the oven and bake for a further 15 minutes or until the cheese has melted and is bubbling. Serve the pie hot.

CREAMY FISH AND PUMPKIN PIE

PREPARATION TIME 10 minutes
COOKING TIME 30 minutes
FREEZING Not suitable

SERVES 4   395 CALS/SERVING

- *700 g (1½ lb) pumpkin or squash, peeled, deseeded and chopped*
- *salt and pepper*
- *350 g (12 oz) courgettes, roughly chopped*
- *450 g (1 lb) cod fillet, skinned and cut into large chunks*
- *125 ml (4 fl oz) milk*
- *3 peppercorns*
- *1 bay leaf*
- *30 ml (2 tbsp) butter or margarine*
- *45 ml (3 tbsp) white plain flour*
- *50 ml (2 fl oz) dry white wine*
- *75 g (3 oz) soft cheese with garlic and herbs*
- *30 ml (2 tbsp) chopped fresh tarragon or 5 ml (1 tsp) dried*
- *4 sheets filo pastry, about 50 g (2 oz) total weight*
- *15 ml (1 tbsp) melted butter or margarine*
- *15 ml (1 tbsp) sesame seeds*

1 Simmer the pumpkin in salted water for 5 minutes. Add the courgettes and simmer for a further 5 minutes or until just tender. Drain well.
2 Meanwhile, place the cod in a saucepan with the milk, peppercorns, bay leaf and 125 ml (4 fl oz) water and simmer for about 2 minutes until just tender. Drain well, reserving the cooking liquid.
3 Melt the butter in a saucepan, add the flour and cook gently for 1 minute, stirring. Remove from the heat and gradually stir in 275 ml (9 fl oz) reserved cooking liquid and the wine. Bring to the boil and cook, stirring, until the sauce thickens. Remove from the heat and stir in the cheese and tarragon. Season to taste.
4 Place the vegetables and fish in a 1.1 litre (2 pint) ovenproof dish. Spoon over the sauce. Crumple pastry on top and brush with melted butter. Sprinkle with sesame seeds.
5 Bake at 200°C (400°F) mark 6 for about 15 minutes until golden brown and piping hot.

PAN-FRIED COD WITH CHANTERELLE MUSHROOMS

PREPARATION TIME 20 minutes
COOKING TIME About 20 minutes
FREEZING Not suitable

SERVES 4

- *4 slices white bread*
- *4 cod steaks, each weighing about 175 g (6 oz)*
- *75 g (3 oz) butter*
- *30 ml (2 tbsp) vegetable oil*
- *salt and pepper*
- *plain flour for dredging*
- *4 spring onions, finely chopped*

480 CALS/SERVING

- *225 g (8 oz) chanterelle mushrooms or mixed mushrooms*
- *1 garlic clove, peeled and crushed*
- *45 ml (3 tbsp) crème fraîche*
- *30 ml (2 tbsp) chopped fresh chives*

1 Remove the crusts from the bread and cut the slices into ovals, the same size as the cod steaks. Heat half the butter and the oil in a frying pan. Fry the bread slices on both sides until crisp and golden. Keep warm.
2 Season the cod, then coat with flour. Heat the remaining butter in the frying pan and fry the cod for about 5 minutes on each side until cooked through and lightly golden. Remove from the pan and keep warm.
3 Add the spring onions, mushrooms and garlic to the pan and sauté for 5 minutes until the juices are just beginning to escape from the mushrooms. Stir in the crème fraîche and heat through gently. Season and add half the chives.
4 Place a bread croûte on each plate, arrange a cod steak on top and spoon the mushroom mixture on top of the fish. Sprinkle with the remaining chives and serve at once.

NOTE Any other variety of wild mushroom can be used instead of chanterelles.

4 Cook under the grill for 4-5 minutes on each side, or until cooked and caramelized. Remove cocktail sticks.
5 Serve immediately on a bed of salad leaves and garnished with lime wedges and chopped red chilli, with the sweet and sour sauce poured over.

HADDOCK AND CORN CHOWDER

PREPARATION TIME 20 minutes
COOKING TIME About 20 minutes
FREEZING Not suitable

SERVES 4   430 CALS/SERVING

- *25-50 g (1-2 oz) butter or margarine*
- *450 g (1 lb) old potatoes, peeled and diced*
- *225 g (8 oz) onion, peeled and thinly sliced*
- *2.5 ml (½ tsp) chilli powder*
- *600 ml (1 pint) vegetable stock*
- *600 ml (1 pint) milk*
- *salt and pepper*

- *225 g (8 oz) fresh haddock fillet, skinned and broken into bite-sized pieces*
- *225 g (8 oz) smoked haddock fillet, skinned and broken into bite-sized pieces*
- *200 g (7 oz) can sweetcorn kernels*
- *125 g (4 oz) cooked peeled prawns*
- *chopped fresh parsley*

m1 Heat the butter in a large saucepan and fry the vegetables and the chilli powder for 2-3 minutes until beginning to soften.
2 Pour in the stock and milk with a little seasoning. Bring to the boil, then cover and simmer for 10 minutes.
3 Add the haddock to the pan with the corn. Return to the boil, then cover and simmer until the potatoes are tender and the fish begins to flake apart. Skim the surface as necessary.
4 Stir in the prawns with plenty of parsley. Adjust the seasoning and serve at once.

VARIATION This hearty, meal-in-a-bowl chowder is equally delicious made with other fish. You can use cod or whiting, or fresh salmon if you are feeling extravagant. For extra colour, sauté a finely diced red pepper with the other vegetables.

THAI GRILLED CARAMELIZED FISH

PREPARATION TIME 15 minutes, plus standing
COOKING TIME 30 minutes
FREEZING Not suitable

SERVES 4   375 CALS/SERVING

- *4 whole plaice fillets, skinned and halved*
- *5 ml (1 tsp) salt*
- *juice of 2 limes*
- *60-90 ml (4-6 tbsp) demerara sugar*
- *salad leaves, lime wedges and 5 ml (1 tsp) finely chopped red chilli, to garnish*

SWEET AND SOUR CHILLI SAUCE
- *400 g (14 oz) red peppers, deseeded and chopped*

- *50 g (2 oz) red chillies, deseeded and chopped*
- *2 garlic cloves, peeled and chopped*
- *30 ml (2 tbsp) olive oil*
- *60 ml (4 tbsp) sugar*
- *90 ml (6 tbsp) distilled malt vinegar*

1 First make the sauce. Place the peppers, chillies and garlic in a blender or food processor with 30 ml (2 tbsp) water and blend until smooth.
2 Put the remaining ingredients in a saucepan and add the chilli paste with 125 ml (4 fl oz) water. Bring to the boil and simmer for about 20 minutes or until reduced by half.
3 Meanwhile, sprinkle each half-fillet with salt and lime juice and roll up. Secure with wooden cocktail sticks. Set aside for 30 minutes. Just before grilling, rub fish all over with the sugar.

PLAICE WITH GRAPES

PREPARATION TIME 30 minutes
COOKING TIME 25 minutes
FREEZING Not suitable
♡

SERVES 4

- *175 g (6 oz) green grapes, skinned, halved and deseeded*
- *8 large plaice fillets, each weighing about 125 g (4 oz), skinned*
- *125 ml (4 fl oz) dry white wine*
- *125 ml (4 fl oz) fish stock*
- *10 ml (2 tsp) finely chopped fresh basil or 5 ml (1 tsp) dried basil*

270 CALS/SERVING

- *2-3 bay leaves*
- *5 ml (1 tsp) cornflour*
- *125 ml (4 fl oz) milk*
- *salt and pepper*
- *30 ml (2 tbsp) Greek yogurt*
- *chopped fresh parsley, to garnish*

1 Place 2-3 grape halves on the skinned side of each plaice fillet. Roll up from the narrow end, secure with cocktail sticks and arrange close together in a poaching pan or large saucepan.
2 Mix together the wine, stock, basil and bay leaves and pour over the fish. Bring to the boil, lower the heat, cover and poach gently for 10 minutes until the fish is cooked.
3 Using a slotted spoon, transfer the fish rolls to a serving dish, draining well. Remove the cocktail sticks if wished, and keep warm. Simmer the cooking liquid for about 10 minutes to reduce by half. Remove the bay leaves.
4 Blend the cornflour with the milk, then stir into the cooking liquid. Season and bring back to the boil, stirring continuously until slightly thickened. Simmer for a further 5 minutes to give a pouring consistency. Stir in the yogurt.
5 Add the remaining grapes. Pour the sauce over the fish rolls and sprinkle with parsley. Serve at once.

TIP
To make skinning grapes an easier task, nick each one with a sharp knife and cover with boiling water for 30 seconds. Then drain and peel away the skins.

PAN-ROASTED MONKFISH WITH SWEET POTATOES AND ONIONS

PREPARATION TIME 20 minutes
COOKING TIME 40-45 minutes
FREEZING Not suitable

SERVES 4
- *700 g (1½ lb) monkfish tail, skinned*
- *50 g (2 oz) can anchovies in oil, drained and washed*
- *salt and pepper*
- *4 slices Parma ham*
- *juice of ½ lemon*
- *700 g (1½ lb) sweet potatoes, scrubbed*

490 CALS/SERVING
- *2 red onions, peeled and cut into wedges*
- *12 whole garlic cloves, peeled*
- *2 sprigs rosemary*
- *60 ml (4 tbsp) olive oil*
- *225 g (8 oz) baby tomatoes*
- *tapenade (black olive paste), to serve*

TIP
If preferred, ask your fishmonger to fillet the fish for you.

1 Wash and dry the monkfish and, using a sharp knife, cut down each side of the bone and discard. Arrange the fillets back together and place the anchovy fillets in the gap left by the bone. Season with pepper.
2 Wrap the Parma ham around the fish and secure with cocktail sticks. Squeeze over the lemon juice and set aside.
3 Cut the potatoes into wedges and place in a large roasting pan with the onions, garlic and rosemary sprigs. Season well and stir in the olive oil. Transfer to the oven and roast at 230°C (450°F) mark 8 on the top shelf for 15 minutes.
4 Remove the pan from the oven and arrange the monkfish tail well down amongst the vegetables. Arrange the tomatoes on top of the vegetables, return to the oven and roast for a further 25-30 minutes until the fish is firm to the touch and the vegetables are tender.
5 Cover with foil and allow to rest for 5 minutes before slicing and serving the fish with the roasted vegetables and a little tapenade.

VARIATION For a Mediterranean flavour, spread olive paste along the centre of the fish with the anchovies and roast with red peppers, aubergines and courgettes as well as the garlic and onions.

ROAST SALMON WITH A PEANUT CRUST

PREPARATION TIME 5 minutes
COOKING TIME 20 minutes
FREEZING Suitable (stage 2)
🕐 ❄

SERVES 4   865 CALS/SERVING

- *1 red chilli, finely chopped*
- *2.5 cm (1 inch) piece fresh root ginger, peeled and grated*
- *175 g (6 oz) unsalted butter, softened*
- *45 ml (3 tbsp) chopped fresh parsley*
- *finely grated rind of 1 lime*
- *75 g (3 oz) salted roasted peanuts*
- *3-4 spring onions, trimmed and finely chopped*
- *125 g (4 oz) fresh white breadcrumbs*
- *salt and pepper*
- *4 salmon fillets, about 175 g (6 oz) each (skinned if wished)*

1 Beat the red chilli and the ginger into the unsalted butter with the fresh parsley and lime rind. Roughly process the peanuts in a blender or food processor.

2 Melt 50 g (2 oz) of the flavoured butter in a frying pan, add the spring onions, peanuts and breadcrumbs and fry until golden, stirring continuously to prevent the breadcrumbs from sticking together. Season to taste.

3 Arrange the salmon fillets, skin-side uppermost, in a roasting tin. Spoon the fried breadcrumb mixture on the top. Cook at 200°C (400°F) mark 6 for 10-15 minutes or until the salmon is just cooked.

4 Melt the remaining flavoured butter and serve with the roast salmon.

TIP

To save cooking time, make up a batch of the spicy flavoured butter and the fried peanut and breadcrumb topping, and freeze ahead. Both of these mixtures can be used direct from the freezer; just allow an extra 2-3 minutes cooking time at stage 3.

PAN-FRIED RED MULLET WITH CITRUS AND BASIL

PREPARATION TIME 10 minutes, plus marinating
COOKING TIME 10 minutes
FREEZING Not suitable

SERVES 4   430 CALS/SERVING

- *4 red mullet, each about 225 g (8 oz), filleted*
- *90 ml (6 tbsp) olive oil*
- *10 peppercorns, crushed*
- *2 oranges*
- *1 lemon*
- *30 ml (2 tbsp) plain flour*
- *salt and peppet*
- *15 g (½ oz) butter*
- *2 anchovies*
- *15 g (½ oz) shredded fresh basil*

1 Place the fish fillets in a shallow dish, in a single layer. Drizzle over the olive oil and sprinkle with the peppercorns. Peel one of the oranges, removing all of the skin and white pith, then cut into thin slices. Lay the orange slices over the fish. Cover and leave to marinate in the refrigerator for 4 hours.

2 Halve the lemon. Remove the skin and white pith from one half, then slice thinly. Squeeze the juice from the other half and reserve.

3 Using a fish slice lift the fish out of the marinade, reserving the marinade, and pat dry on absorbent kitchen paper. Season with salt and pepper, then dust lightly with flour.

4 Heat 45 ml (3 tbsp) of the marinade in a sauté pan or frying pan. Add the red mullet fillets and fry for 2 minutes on each side. Remove from the pan and set aside; keep warm. Discard the oil remaining in the pan.

5 Melt the butter in the pan with the remaining marinade. Add the anchovies and crush until dissolved. Add the juice of the remaining orange and the reserved lemon juice. Season and cook until slightly reduced. Lastly, stir in the shredded basil.

6 Pour the citrus sauce over the fish and garnish with the orange and lemon slices. Serve at once.

150 ml (5 fl oz) of the hot stock and cook, stirring constantly, until the liquid is absorbed by the rice. Continue adding stock in 150 ml (5 fl oz) quantities until you have used half of it. This should take about 10 minutes and the rice should be about half cooked.

3 Stir in the seafood and cook for 2-3 minutes. Continue adding the stock as before, until the rice is tender but with a firm bite (you may not need to add all the stock). The rice should hold together in a creamy mass.

4 Stir in the lemon rind, tomato paste and tarragon. Season with salt and pepper to taste and leave to stand for a few minutes before serving.

NOTE Arborio rice is the classic Italian risotto rice and produces a delicious creamy texture. Ready-prepared mixed seafood is sold in packets from most supermarkets.

VARIATION If preferred, make the risotto with one type of seafood only, such as prawns or mussels. You can also vary the herbs used.

SEAFOOD RISOTTO

PREPARATION TIME 10 minutes
COOKING TIME 30 minutes
FREEZING Not suitable

SERVES 4
- *60 ml (4 tbsp) sunflower oil*
- *1 onion, peeled and finely chopped*
- *2 garlic cloves, peeled and crushed*
- *225 g (8 oz) Arborio rice*
- *100 ml (3½ fl oz) dry white wine*
- *1.5-1.6 litres (2¼-2½ pints) hot fish stock*

420 CALS/SERVING
- *300 g (10 oz) prepared mixed seafood*
- *grated rind of 1 small lemon*
- *30 ml (2 tbsp) sun-dried tomato paste*
- *15 ml (1 tbsp) chopped fresh tarragon*
- *salt and pepper*

1 Heat the oil in a heavy-based pan, add the onion and garlic and cook until softened. Add the rice and cook, stirring, for about 1 minute.

2 Add the wine and stir until it is absorbed. Add

MUSSELS IN TOMATO SAUCE

PREPARATION TIME 5 minutes
COOKING TIME About 10 minutes
FREEZING Not suitable
♡ ⏲

SERVES 4
- *45 ml (3 tbsp) olive oil*
- *1 onion, peeled and finely chopped*
- *2 garlic cloves, peeled and crushed*
- *700g (1½ lb) plum tomatoes, peeled, deseeded and chopped*

260 CALS/SERVING
- *5 ml (1 tsp) sugar*
- *45 ml (3 tbsp) chopped fresh oregano*
- *salt and pepper*
- *15 ml (1 tbsp) tomato purée*
- *450 g (1 lb) shelled cooked mussels*

1 Heat the oil in a saucepan, add the onion and cook for 5 minutes until softened. Stir in the garlic, tomatoes, sugar and half the oregano. Season with salt and pepper to taste and simmer gently for 2-3 minutes until the tomatoes soften.

2 Stir in the tomato purée, add the mussels and simmer for 1-2 minutes until heated through. Scatter the remaining oregano over and serve hot.

CHARRED SCALLOPS WITH FENNEL AND PERNOD

PREPARATION TIME 10 minutes
COOKING TIME 10-15 minutes
FREEZING Not suitable

SERVES 4

- *1 large fennel bulb, about 225 g (8 oz)*
- *50 g (2 oz) butter*
- *4 shallots, peeled and chopped*
- *2 garlic cloves, peeled and crushed*

415 CALS/SERVING

- *30 ml (2 tbsp) Pernod*
- *90 ml (3 fl oz) double cream*
- *oil for frying*
- *salt and pepper*
- *12-16 shelled scallops*

1 Trim the green feathery tops from the fennel. Reserve a few tops for garnishing and chop the remainder – you need 15 ml (1 tbsp) chopped tops. Slice the fennel bulb.

2 Heat the butter in a small saucepan, add the shallots and garlic and cook for 3 minutes until soft. Add the Pernod and cream and cook gently for 2-3 minutes. Stir in the chopped fennel tops.

3 Heat a heavy-based ridged frying pan or griddle pan with a little oil until very hot and just smoking. Turn down the heat a little, then place the fennel slices on the frying pan or griddle and cook for a few minutes on each side until slightly charred. Transfer to a warmed serving plate and keep warm.

4 Gently reheat the sauce and season with salt and pepper to taste.

5 Meanwhile, place the scallops on the frying pan or griddle and cook for 1-2 minutes on each side until slightly charred. Transfer to the serving plate of cooked fennel, garnish with the reserved fennel tops and serve at once with the hot sauce.

TIP

Serve the cooked scallops and fennel in scrubbed scallop shells for an attractive presentation.

CHICKEN AND APPLE CASSEROLE

PREPARATION TIME 20 minutes
COOKING TIME 1 hour 10 minutes
FREEZING Not suitable

SERVES 4   440 CALS/SERVING
- *30 ml (2 tbsp) olive oil*
- *4 chicken quarters, about 900 g (2 lb) total weight*
- *900 g (2 lb) mixed seasonal root vegetables, peeled and sliced*
- *350 g (12 oz) onion, peeled and roughly chopped*
- *125 g (4 oz) green lentils*
- *2 small eating apples, peeled, cored and sliced*
- *200 ml (7 fl oz) apple juice*
- *300 ml (10 fl oz) chicken stock*
- *salt and pepper*

1 Heat the oil in a large flameproof casserole, add the chicken quarters and brown well. Remove from the pan with a slotted spoon and drain on absorbent kitchen paper.
2 Add all the vegetables to the pan and sauté for 4-5 minutes or until beginning to colour. Add the lentils, sliced apples, apple juice and chicken stock and bring to the boil. Season well and replace the chicken quarters.
3 Cover and cook at 190°C (375°F) mark 5 for about 50 minutes or until the chicken and lentils are tender and cooked through. Adjust the seasoning before serving.

VARIATIONS You can add any of your favourite seasonal root vegetables to this casserole – just keep the total weight the same. If you prefer a casserole with thicker juices, simply purée some of the vegetables and stir back in.

TIP
If you want to prepare the apples slightly in advance, place the slices in cold water mixed with lemon juice as you cut them up. This will stop the flesh from discolouring.

SPICY COCONUT CHICKEN

PREPARATION TIME 10 minutes
COOKING TIME 35 minutes
FREEZING Not suitable
♡

SERVES 6   270 CALS/SERVING

- *6 chicken breast fillets with skin, about 700 g (1½ lb) total weight*
- *45 ml (3 tbsp) vegetable oil*
- *225 g (8 oz) onion, peeled and finely chopped*
- *1 garlic clove, peeled and crushed*
- *1 cm (½ inch) piece fresh root ginger, peeled and finely chopped*
- *2.5 ml (½ tsp) ground turmeric*
- *5 ml (1 tsp) each ground cumin, ground coriander and mild curry powder*
- *pinch hot chilli powder (optional)*
- *225 g (8 oz) can chopped tomatoes*
- *75 g (3 oz) creamed coconut, coarsely grated*
- *30 ml (2 tbsp) poppy seeds*
- *300 ml (10 fl oz) chicken stock*
- *salt and pepper*
- *30 ml (2 tbsp) Greek natural yogurt*
- *chopped fresh coriander, to garnish*

1 Tuck the ends of the chicken breasts under to shape into neat rounds; tie with string.
2 Heat the oil in a pan and sauté the chicken fillets until golden. Remove with a slotted spoon and drain on absorbent kitchen paper.
3 Add the onion, garlic and ginger and cook, stirring, for 1-2 minutes. Add the spices. Cook for a further minute, then add the tomatoes, coconut and poppy seeds. Cook for a further minute, add the stock, then bring to the boil and simmer for 2-3 minutes.
4 Replace the chicken, cover and simmer for about 20 minutes or until the chicken is cooked through.
5 Skim off any excess oil and adjust the seasoning. Off the heat, stir in the yogurt. Serve garnished with fresh coriander.

ORIENTAL CHICKEN PARCELS

PREPARATION TIME 20 minutes, plus marinating
COOKING TIME 35 minutes
FREEZING Not suitable
♡

SERVES 4   215 CALS/SERVING

- *3 oranges*
- *juice of 1 lemon*
- *30 ml (2 tbsp) dark soy sauce*
- *30 ml (2 tbsp) yellow bean sauce*
- *15 ml (1 tbsp) dry sherry*
- *15 ml (1 tbsp) vegetable oil*
- *salt and pepper*
- *four 125 g (4 oz) skinless chicken breast fillets*
- *50 g (2 oz) stem ginger or 2.5 cm (1 inch) piece fresh root ginger, peeled and thinly sliced*
- *1 bunch spring onions, trimmed and shredded*
- *125 g (4 oz) carrots, peeled and shredded*

1 In a bowl mix together the finely grated rind of one orange with 60 ml (4 tbsp) orange juice, the lemon juice, soy sauce, yellow bean sauce, sherry and oil. Season well with salt and pepper.
2 Lightly slash the chicken breasts all over and stir into the marinade with the ginger, spring onions and carrot. Refrigerate overnight.
3 The next day, segment the remaining oranges. Cut four 30 cm (12 inch) squares of foil and pull up the edges to make open purses. Divide the chicken and marinade among the foil pieces and top with orange segments. Pinch the corners of the foil together. Place the parcels in a roasting tin.
4 Cook at 180°C (350°F) mark 4 for about 35 minutes or until the chicken is tender. Open the parcels into soup bowls to serve as there is quite a lot of juice.

SOUTHERN FRIED CHICKEN WITH CORN FRITTERS

PREPARATION TIME 15 minutes
COOKING TIME 20 minutes
FREEZING Not suitable

SERVES 4-6   660-440 CALS/SERVING

- 6 *allspice berries*
- 10 *black peppercorns*
- 40 g (1½ oz) *white plain flour*
- 1 *garlic clove, peeled and finely chopped*
- 2.5 ml (½ tsp) *dried thyme*
- *salt and pepper*
- 8-12 *chicken drumsticks, skinned*
- 1 *egg, beaten*
- 125-175 g (4-6 oz) *dried breadcrumbs*
- *vegetable oil for frying*

CORN FRITTERS
- 75 g (3 oz) *white plain flour*
- 1 *egg*
- 75 ml (3 fl oz) *milk*

- 200 g (7 oz) *can sweetcorn, drained*
- 2 *spring onions, trimmed and finely chopped*

TOMATO SALSA
- 6 *ripe tomatoes, cored and finely chopped*
- 1 *red onion, peeled and finely chopped*
- 1 *spring onion, trimmed and finely chopped*
- ¼ *cucumber, finely chopped*
- *a little olive oil*
- *dash of wine vinegar*
- *chopped fresh chives, basil or coriander*

1 First make the tomato salsa. Mix the tomatoes with the chopped onions and cucumber, moistening with a little olive oil and vinegar. Season liberally with salt and pepper. Add chopped herbs to taste.
2 For the chicken, crush the allspice berries and peppercorns together, using a pestle and mortar. Mix the flour with the allspice mixture, garlic, thyme and plenty of salt. Toss the chicken in the flour mixture to coat evenly.
3 Dip each chicken portion first in the beaten egg, and then in the breadcrumbs to coat. Arrange in a single layer on a plate and chill while making the corn fritters.
4 To make the corn fritters, put the flour and a large pinch of salt into a bowl and make a well in the centre. Add the egg and milk and beat thoroughly to make a smooth thick batter. Fold the sweetcorn and spring onion into the batter.
5 Heat a little oil in a frying pan and fry a few large spoonfuls of the sweetcorn batter mixture for 2-3 minutes each side until golden brown and crisp. Drain on absorbent kitchen paper and keep warm in a hot oven while you cook the remainder. (There should be sufficient to make 12 fritters.)
6 Meanwhile heat the oil for deep frying in a deep-fat fryer to 170°C (325°F). Fry the chicken, in batches, for about 10 minutes until crisp and golden and cooked right through. Keep warm with the corn fritters.
7 Serve the chicken and corn fritters as soon as they are all cooked, with the salsa.

CHICKEN BREASTS WITH APPLE AND THYME

PREPARATION TIME 15 minutes
COOKING TIME 1 hour
FREEZING Not suitable
♡

SERVES 4   330 CALS/SERVING

- 50 g (2 oz) *butter*
- 175 g (6 oz) *onion, peeled and chopped*
- 2 *crisp dessert apples*
- 50 g (2 oz) *mature Cheddar cheese*
- 40 g (1½ oz) *fresh breadcrumbs*
- 30 ml (2 tbsp) *chopped fresh thyme or 5 ml (1 tsp) dried*
- *salt and pepper*

- 4 *chicken breast fillets with skin, about 700 g (1½ lb) total weight*
- 75 ml (3 fl oz) *apple juice*
- 20 ml (4 tsp) *cornflour*
- 300 ml (10 fl oz) *chicken stock*
- 15 ml (1 tbsp) *wholegrain mustard*

1 Heat 25 g (1 oz) butter in a frying pan and sauté the onion until softened. Leave to cool. Grate the apples and cheese into the onion. Add the breadcrumbs, thyme and seasoning.
2 Loosen the skin of the chicken and push the stuffing underneath, pressing into place. Place in a roasting tin, dot with the remaining butter and season. Pour the apple juice over.
3 Cook at 190°C (375°F) mark 5 for about 50 minutes or until cooked through. Remove the chicken from the pan and keep warm.
4 Blend the cornflour with 30 ml (2 tbsp) cold water, add to the pan with the stock and mustard, bring to the boil, stirring, and cook for 2-3 minutes. Season and spoon over the chicken.

GARLIC CHICKEN WITH
ROAST PEPPER PUREE

PREPARATION TIME 20 minutes, plus marinating
COOKING TIME 1 hour and 5 minutes
FREEZING Not suitable

SERVES 6

- 6 skinless chicken breast fillets
- 4 garlic cloves, peeled and crushed
- 15 ml (1 tbsp) chopped fresh thyme
- 105 ml (7 tbsp) olive oil
- 15 ml (1 tbsp) clear honey
- 15 ml (1 tbsp) white wine vinegar
- salt and pepper
- 4 red peppers, deseeded

420 CALS/SERVING

- 2 yellow peppers, deseeded
- 2 onions, peeled and sliced
- 225 g (8 oz) plum tomatoes, skinned and halved
- 10 ml (2 tsp) paprika
- 15 ml (1 tbsp) tomato purée
- thyme sprigs, to garnish

1 Cut several deep slits across each chicken breast and lay them in a large shallow dish. Scatter the garlic over the chicken with the chopped thyme. Mix 30 ml (2 tbsp) oil with the honey and wine vinegar. Season and pour over the chicken. Leave to marinate for several hours.

2 Drain the chicken, reserving the marinade juices. Heat 30 ml (2 tbsp) olive oil in a frying pan. Add the chicken, slit sides down, and fry quickly to sear. Turn the chicken and cook for a further minute. Transfer to a shallow baking dish with a slotted spoon.

3 Cut each pepper into 8 chunks. Place the onions, peppers and tomatoes in a large shallow ovenproof dish. Sprinkle with the paprika and pour over the remaining oil.

4 Bake the vegetables at 200°C (400°F) mark 6, near the top of the oven, for 1 hour, until lightly charred. Halfway through cooking, place the chicken on a lower shelf and bake for 30 minutes until cooked through.

5 Reserve 6 pieces of red pepper and 6 pieces of yellow pepper for garnish – cut into strips and keep warm. Place the remaining vegetable mixture in a food processor or blender and blend until almost smooth. Place in a saucepan and heat through, adding the tomato purée and seasoning to taste.

6 Spoon the pepper purée onto warmed serving plates and top with the chicken breasts and reserved peppers. Garnish with thyme sprigs and serve.

a little at a time, until melted. Simmer, stirring constantly, until the sauce has reduced and thickened. Taste and adjust the seasoning, adding more sugar if the sauce seems too tart.

3 Heat the butter and oil in a large frying pan and pan-fry the steaks for 3-4 minutes on each side. Stir in the sauce with the reserved blueberries and heat through. Serve garnished with orange slices and coriander sprigs.

PAN-FRIED VENISON WITH BLUEBERRY SAUCE

PREPARATION TIME 15 minutes
COOKING TIME About 15 minutes
FREEZING Sauce only (stage 1)
♡ ◷ ✳

SERVES 6

- *15 g (½ oz) butter*
- *15 ml (1 tbsp) vegetable oil*
- *6 venison steaks, each weighing 125-175 g (4-6 oz)*
- *orange slices and sprigs of coriander, to garnish*
BLUEBERRY SAUCE
- *225 g (8 oz) blueberries*

250 CALS/SERVING

- *150 ml (5 fl oz) dry white wine*
- *10 ml (2 tsp) caster sugar, or to taste*
- *60 ml (4 tbsp) freshly squeezed orange juice*
- *15 ml (1 tbsp) wine vinegar*
- *salt and pepper*
- *25 g (1 oz) unsalted butter*

1 To make the blueberry sauce, reserve about one quarter of the blueberries and put the remainder in a heavy saucepan with the white wine and sugar. Bring to the boil, stirring, then cover and simmer for 10 minutes until the berries are soft, stirring occasionally. Remove from the heat and work through a sieve into a jug.

2 Return the puréed blueberries to the pan and add the orange juice, vinegar and salt and pepper to taste. Bring to the boil, then whisk in the butter,

COUNTRY-STYLE RABBIT CASSEROLE

PREPARATION TIME 10 minutes
COOKING TIME 1¾ hours
FREEZING Suitable
♡ ✳

SERVES 6

- *45 ml (3 tbsp) olive oil*
- *1.1 kg (2½ lb) rabbit pieces*
- *1 large onion, peeled and sliced*
- *2 garlic cloves, peeled and crushed*
- *125 g (4 oz) lean smoked bacon, diced*
- *30 ml (2 tbsp) brandy*
- *200 ml (7 fl oz) white wine*

335 CALS/SERVING

- *400 g (14 oz) can chopped tomatoes*
- *2.5 ml (½ tsp) dried thyme*
- *15 ml (1 tbsp) chopped fresh parsley*
- *salt and pepper*
- *50 g (2 oz) brown cap mushrooms, sliced*
- *chopped flat-leaf parsley, to garnish*

1 Heat the oil in a heavy-based flameproof casserole. Add the rabbit pieces and brown well on all sides. Remove with a slotted spoon.

2 Add the onion, garlic and bacon to the casserole. Gently fry until the onion has softened. Return the rabbit to the casserole.

3 Warm the brandy gently in a small pan or ladle. Remove the casserole from the heat, pour the brandy over the rabbit and set it alight.

4 When the flames have died down, return the casserole to the heat and add the wine, tomatoes, thyme and parsley. Season with salt and pepper. Cover and simmer over a low heat for about 1½ hours, adding the mushrooms 10 minutes before the end of the cooking time. Serve garnished with chopped parsley.

RAISED GAME PIE

PREPARATION TIME 1¼ hours, plus resting and chilling
COOKING TIME 1 hour 55 minutes
FREEZING Suitable (stage 9)

❄

SERVES 8-10

*HOT WATER CRUST
PASTRY*
- *300 g (10 oz) white
  plain flour*
- *1.25 ml (¼ tsp) salt*
- *65 g (2½ oz) white
  vegetable fat*
PIE FILLING
- *225 g (8 oz) rabbit
  joints, skinned*
- *225 g (8 oz) shoulder
  venison*
- *1.1 litres (2 pints)
  brown stock*
- *225 g (8 oz) pork
  sausagemeat*
- *½ onion, peeled and
  finely chopped*
- *2 garlic cloves,
  peeled and crushed*

440-355 CALS/SERVING
- *60 ml (4 tbsp)
  Madeira*
- *2.5 ml (½ tsp)
  ground mace*
- *salt and pepper*
- *125 g (4 oz) no-soak
  dried apricots*
- *4 no-soak prunes*
- *2 pheasant or
  chicken breasts,
  boned and skinned,
  about 225 g (8 oz)
  total weight*
- *8 large sage leaves
  or 5 ml (1 tsp) dried
  sage*
- *beaten egg, to glaze*
- *5 ml (1 tsp)
  powdered gelatine*

1 For the filling, remove the flesh from the rabbit joints. Cut the rabbit and venison into small pieces. Place in a saucepan and cover with the stock. Bring to the boil, cover and simmer for 25 minutes, or until tender; drain and cool. Reduce the stock by boiling to 150 ml (5 fl oz).

2 Base-line a 25 x 7.5 cm (10 x 3 inch) loose-sided pie mould with non-stick baking parchment. Mix the cooled meats, sausagemeat, onion, garlic, Madeira, mace and seasoning. Cover and chill.

3 To prepare the hot water crust pastry, sift the flour and salt into a bowl and make a well in the centre. Heat the fat and 125-150 ml (4-5 fl oz) water gently together until the fat melts, then bring to the boil and pour into the well.

4 Gradually lap the flour into the liquid, then beat together. Lightly knead against the side of the bowl until smooth. Immediately wrap the pastry in a tea towel. (If exposed to the air, it will become dry and impossible to use.) Leave for up to 30 minutes; no longer. Use warm.

5 On a lightly floured surface, roll out three quarters of the pastry to an oblong 20 x 35 cm (8 x 14 inches), turning to keep an even shape and thickness.

Use the rolling pin to help lift pastry over the tin. (Keep the remaining pastry covered on a plate placed over warm water.)

6 Ease the pastry into the corners and press evenly up the sides of the tin. Trim off excess pastry. Line with baking parchment and beans and bake blind at 200°C (400°F) mark 6 for 15-20 minutes, until golden brown and set. Remove paper and beans. Allow to cool.

7 Spoon half the meat mixture into the pastry case. Scissor-snip half the apricots and 2 prunes into the tin. Place the pheasant or chicken breasts end to end over the fruit. Place the sage leaves on top. Repeat the fruit and meat layers.

8 Roll out the remaining pastry to a 28 x 10 cm (11 x 4 inch) oblong and use to top the pie. Seal well, then trim and flute the edges. Make a small hole in the centre of the pie, and two more near the edge. Shape the pastry trimmings into leaf and berry shapes. Arrange on top of the pie, half covering the holes.

9 Place the pie on a baking tray and glaze with egg. Bake at 200°C (400°F) mark 6 for 20 minutes, then reduce the temperature to 180°C (350°F) mark 4 and cook for a further 1¼ hours, covering the top lightly with foil if necessary. Ease away the sides of the tin and bake the pie for a further 20 minutes to brown the sides. Cool.

10 Soak the gelatine in 20 ml (4 tsp) water, then dissolve in the stock. Chill until beginning to set. Place the pie on a large edged plate, easing off the base gently. Gradually pour in the stock through the holes. Cover loosely, then refrigerate overnight.

CASSEROLE OF GROUSE WITH RED WINE

PREPARATION TIME 10 minutes
COOKING TIME 1¼ hours
FREEZING Suitable
♡ ❄

SERVES 4   300 CALS/SERVING
- *2 brace of grouse*
- *about 45 ml (3 tbsp) vegetable oil*
- *450 g (1 lb) shallots or button onions, peeled*
- *4 large celery sticks, sliced*
- *200 ml (7 fl oz) red wine*

- *2 bay leaves*
- *salt and pepper*
- *200 ml (7 fl oz) stock*
- *15 ml (1 tbsp) arrowroot*
- *15 ml (1 tbsp) lemon juice*
- *chopped parsley, to garnish*

1 Wipe the grouse, trim the feet and remove any feather ends. Heat the oil in a flameproof casserole and brown the birds well, in batches if necessary. Lift out of the casserole using a slotted spoon.
2 Add the shallots and celery to the casserole with a little extra oil, if necessary, and brown lightly.
3 Pour in the wine and bring to the boil. Add the bay leaves and seasoning and return the grouse to the casserole.
4 Cover tightly and cook at 170°C (325°F) mark 3 for about 50 minutes or until the grouse are just tender. Lift the birds out of the casserole, cover and keep warm.
5 Add the stock to the casserole and warm slightly. Mix the arrowroot to a smooth paste with a little water and stir into the casserole. Bring to the boil, stirring, and cook until slightly thickened. Stir in the lemon juice, adjust the seasoning and spoon over the birds. Garnish with parsley to serve.

FRENCH ROAST PHEASANT WITH GRAPES AND NUTS

PREPARATION TIME 25 minutes
COOKING TIME 1 hour
FREEZING Not suitable

SERVES 6   635 CALS/SERVING
- *6 clementines*
- *700 g (1½ lb) white or red grapes*
- *15 ml (1 tbsp) green tea (Gunpowder or Darjeeling)*
- *200 ml (7 fl oz) Madeira or sweet sherry*
- *2 young oven-ready pheasants*

- *softened butter, for basting*
- *salt and pepper*
- *10 ml (2 tsp) balsamic or sherry vinegar*
- *15 ml (1 tbsp) dark soy sauce*
- *225 g (8 oz) walnut halves*
- *grapes, to garnish*

1 Grate the rind from 2 clementines and squeeze the juice from all six; place in a bowl. Reserve the ungrated squeezed halves. Chop the grapes roughly in a food processor and pour into the clementine juice. Pour 300 ml (10 fl oz) boiling water over the green tea, leave to steep for 5 minutes, then strain and reserve.
2 Pour half the clementine and grape juice into a roasting tin, adding the Madeira and any giblets (except the liver). Place the reserved clementine halves inside the pheasant cavities. Smear the pheasants with butter and season with salt and pepper.
3 Place the birds in the roasting tin on one side. Roast at 200°C (400°F) mark 6 for 45 minutes, turning and basting every 15 minutes until cooked. Test by pushing a skewer into the meatiest part of the thigh; the juices should run clear. Transfer the pheasants to a warmed serving platter and keep warm.
4 Pour the reserved clementine and grape juice into the roasting tin. Stir in the tea, balsamic vinegar and soy sauce. Bring to the boil, scraping up any sediment from the bottom of the pan. Boil for 1-2 minutes, then strain into a saucepan. Stir in the walnuts, bring to the boil and reduce to 450 ml (15 fl oz). Adjust the seasoning. The sauce should be slightly syrupy; if not, reduce a little more. Spoon the walnuts around the pheasant and pour the sauce into a warmed sauceboat. Garnish with extra grapes.

NOTE If your butcher is preparing the birds, ask him to keep the giblets. Or use chicken or turkey giblets.

POT-ROASTED PHEASANT WITH
RED CABBAGE

PREPARATION TIME 20 minutes
COOKING TIME 40 minutes
FREEZING Not suitable

SERVES 4

505 CALS/SERVING

- *25 g (1 oz) butter*
- *15 ml (1 tbsp) vegetable oil*
- *2 oven-ready pheasants, halved*
- *2 onions, peeled and sliced*
- *450 g (1 lb) red cabbage, finely shredded*
- *5 ml (1 tsp) cornflour*
- *250 ml (8 fl oz) red wine*

- *30 ml (2 tbsp) redcurrant jelly*
- *15 ml (1 tbsp) balsamic vinegar*
- *salt and pepper*
- *4 rashers smoked streaky bacon, halved*
- *flat-leaf parsley and bay leaves, to garnish*

1 Melt the butter with the oil in a large flameproof casserole. Add the pheasant halves, and brown on all sides. Remove the pheasant and add the onions and red cabbage to the casserole. Fry for 5 minutes until softened.

2 Blend the cornflour with a little water. Add to the pan with the red wine, redcurrant jelly, vinegar and seasoning. Bring to the boil, stirring.

3 Arrange the pheasant halves, skin-side up, on top of the cabbage. Place the halved bacon rashers on top of the pheasant. Cover with a lid and bake at 200°C (400°F) mark 6 for 30 minutes until tender. Lift out the pheasant halves and keep warm. Using a slotted spoon, divide the cabbage between warmed serving plates. Arrange the pheasant on top and garnish with parsley and bay leaves. Serve any juices in a sauceboat.

VARIATION Pigeon can also be cooked in this way. Use 4 oven-ready pigeons and place a quarter of an onion inside each bird before browning for extra flavour. Tuck the parsley and bay leaf garnish into the cavities for an attractive finish.

BEEF RENDANG

PREPARATION TIME 15 minutes
COOKING TIME About 2 hours 10 minutes
FREEZING Suitable
✳

SERVES 6

- 1 large onion, peeled and quartered
- 6 garlic cloves, peeled
- 5 cm (2 inch) piece fresh root ginger, peeled
- 1 red pepper, deseeded and chopped
- 4 dried hot chillies
- 10 ml (2 tsp) ground coriander
- 10 ml (2 tsp) ground cinnamon
- 5 ml (1 tsp) ground cloves

955 CALS/SERVING

- 5 ml (1 tsp) turmeric
- 45 ml (3 tbsp) vegetable oil
- 1.1 kg (2½ lb) stewing or braising beef, cut into large cubes
- 1.7 litres (3 pints) coconut milk
- 1 lemon grass stalk, bruised
- salt
- finely shredded lime leaves, to garnish (optional)

1 Put the first nine ingredients in a food processor or blender with 15 ml (1 tbsp) water. Process until smooth.
2 Heat the oil in a large, wide flameproof casserole dish or a saucepan. Add the spice paste and cook over a moderate heat for 3-5 minutes, stirring all the time.
3 Add the meat and cook for 2-3 minutes, stirring to coat in the spice mixture.
4 Add the coconut milk and bring to the boil, stirring all the time. Add the lemon grass and about 5 ml (1 tsp) salt. Reduce the heat and simmer very gently, uncovered, for about 2 hours, stirring from time to time. The beef is ready when it is really tender and almost falling apart; the sauce should be well reduced and quite thick.
5 If the sauce is too thin, transfer the meat to a warmed serving dish, using a slotted spoon; keep warm. Bring the sauce to the boil and boil vigorously, stirring frequently, until sufficiently reduced. Pour over the meat. Check the seasoning before serving, garnished with shredded lime leaves, if available.

GRILLED STEAKS WITH SHALLOTS AND WINE

PREPARATION TIME 10 minutes
COOKING TIME 15–25 minutes
FREEZING Not suitable
🕐

SERVES 4

- 50 g (2 oz) chilled butter
- 225 g (8 oz) shallots, peeled and chopped
- 350 ml (12 fl oz) red Bordeaux wine
- 4 sirloin steaks, each weighing about 175-200 g (6-7 oz)
- 30 ml (2 tbsp) vegetable oil

555 CALS/SERVING

- salt and pepper
- 8 slices French bread
- 10-15 ml (2-3 tsp) Dijon mustard
- 30 ml (2 tbsp) chopped fresh parsley
- parsley sprigs, to garnish

1 Melt 15 g (½ oz) of the butter in a saucepan. Add the shallots and sauté for a few minutes until slightly softened. Add the wine and bring to the boil. Simmer, uncovered, until the wine is reduced by half and the shallots are soft.
2 Smear the steaks on both sides with the oil and arrange on the grill rack. Cook, as close to the heat as possible, turning the steaks every 2 minutes. Allow 4 minutes (one turn) for very rare steaks; 8 minutes (three turns) for medium. For well-done steaks allow 12 minutes, increasing the time between turns to 3 minutes. Season the steaks with salt and pepper as you make the final turn.
3 Meanwhile, cut the remaining butter into 6 cubes and beat one at a time into the shallot sauce.
4 Transfer the steaks to warmed serving plates and keep warm. Press the bread slices onto the grill pan to soak up the juices, then spread each lightly with Dijon mustard. Put 2 slices beside each steak. Pour the sauce over the steaks, sprinkle with chopped parsley and serve garnished with sprigs of parsley.

VARIATIONS Use rump rather than sirloin steaks. Use a hot griddle pan to cook the steaks, rather than grill them.

COUNTRY BEEF WITH BARLEY

PREPARATION TIME 15 minutes
COOKING TIME About 2¼ hours
FREEZING Suitable

♡ ❄

SERVES 4

- *450 g (1 lb) braising steak, cubed*
- *salt and pepper*
- *25 g (1 oz) plain flour*
- *15 ml (1 tbsp) vegetable oil*
- *350 g (12 oz) carrots, peeled and chopped*
- *575 g (1¼ lb) swede, peeled and chopped*
- *4 sticks celery, chopped*
- *225 g (8 oz) button onions, peeled*

330 CALS/SERVING

- *1 garlic clove, peeled and crushed*
- *50 g (2 oz) pearl barley*
- *pared rind and juice of 1 orange*
- *150 ml (5 fl oz) red wine*
- *2 large rosemary sprigs or 10 ml (2 tsp) dried*
- *450-600 ml (16-20 fl oz) beef stock*
- *fresh rosemary, to garnish*

1 Toss the beef in seasoned flour until evenly coated. Heat the oil in a 4.2 litre (7 pint) flameproof casserole and brown the beef in batches. Remove with a slotted spoon and drain on absorbent kitchen paper.

2 Lower the heat, add the carrots, swede, celery, onions and garlic, with a little more oil, if necessary. Sauté for 4-5 minutes, stirring occasionally. Return all the beef to the casserole with the pearl barley, orange rind and juice, wine, rosemary and enough stock to cover.

3 Bring to the boil, stir well, cover and cook in the oven at 170°C (325°F) mark 3 for about 2 hours or until the meat is tender. Adjust the seasoning. Serve garnished with fresh rosemary.

MOROCCAN LAMB PIE WITH SPINACH AND SULTANAS

PREPARATION TIME 20 minutes
COOKING TIME 1¼ hours
FREEZING Suitable (stage 3)

❀

SERVES 4

- *15 ml (1 tbsp) oil*
- *175 g (6 oz) onion, peeled and finely chopped*
- *450 g (1 lb) minced lamb*
- *2 garlic cloves, peeled and crushed*
- *5 ml (1 tsp) ground cinnamon*
- *2.5 ml (¹/₂ tsp) ground cloves*
- *10 ml (2 tsp) ground cumin*
- *2.5 ml (¹/₂ tsp) mild curry powder*
- *45 ml (3 tbsp) Worcestershire sauce*
- *30 ml (2 tbsp) red wine*

580 CALS/SERVING

- *15 ml (1 tbsp) tomato purée*
- *50 g (2 oz) sultanas*
- *150 ml (5 fl oz) light stock*
- *225 g (8 oz) frozen leaf spinach, thawed, drained and finely chopped*
- *30 ml (2 tbsp) orange marmalade*
- *30 ml (2 tbsp) chopped fresh parsley*
- *salt and pepper*
- *50 g (2 oz) butter, melted*
- *275 g (10 oz) filo pastry*

1 Heat the oil in a heavy-based flameproof casserole. Sauté the onion, stirring, until it begins to soften and brown. Add the minced lamb and brown thoroughly over high heat, breaking up any lumps of meat.

2 Stir in the garlic with the next seven ingredients and cook for 5 minutes, stirring frequently. Add the sultanas and the stock and bring to the boil.

3 Cover tightly and cook gently for about 20 minutes or until the lamb is tender. Stir once or twice during cooking.

4 Stir the spinach into the casserole with the marmalade and parsley. Adjust the seasoning and leave to cool.

5 Lightly grease a 1.4-1.7 litre (2½-3 pint) shallow ovenproof dish with melted butter. Line with the pastry, buttering between the layers, leaving the edges hanging over the dish. Reserve three or four sheets of pastry. Add the mince mixture. Top with the remaining pastry, brushing with butter, and bring the pastry edges over the top, arranging them randomly. Brush over the remaining butter.

6 Bake at 200°C (400°F) mark 6 for 25 minutes or until golden brown. Cover loosely with foil and cook for a further 15 minutes or until the filling is piping hot.

LAMB CHOPS WITH LEEKS AND LENTILS

PREPARATION TIME 20 minutes, plus marinating
COOKING TIME 30 minutes
FREEZING Not suitable

SERVES 4

- *4 loin lamb chops, each weighing about 125 g (4 oz)*
- *1 small onion, peeled and finely chopped*
- *125 ml (4 fl oz) fresh orange juice*
- *salt and pepper*
- *15 ml (1 tbsp) vegetable oil*
- *450 g (1 lb) leeks, washed, trimmed and cut into 1 cm (1/2 inch) slices*

420 CALS/SERVING

- *125 g (4 oz) split red lentils, boiled rapidly for 10 minutes, then drained*
- *5 ml (1 tsp) paprika*
- *300 ml (10 fl oz) lamb stock*
- *fresh coriander, to garnish*

1 Trim the chops of fat and place in a non-metallic dish. Sprinkle onion and orange juice over the lamb and season with pepper. Cover and refrigerate for at least 12 hours, turning once.
2 Lift the chops out of the marinade and pat dry on absorbent kitchen paper. Heat the oil in a medium-sized frying pan and brown the chops on both sides. Drain on absorbent kitchen paper.
3 Add the leeks, lentils and paprika to the pan and stir over a moderate heat for 1 minute. Place the chops on the lentils. Pour in the marinade and stock and bring to the boil.
4 Cover and simmer for 20 minutes or until the chops are cooked. Adjust the seasoning. Serve garnished with coriander.

> *TIP*
> Fast-boiling pulses for 10 minutes before cooking ensures that any harmful toxins present are destroyed.

SPICED LAMB HOT POT

PREPARATION TIME 30 minutes
COOKING TIME 2½ hours
FREEZING Suitable

❋

SERVES 6

- *about 45 ml (3 tbsp) vegetable oil*
- *900 g (2 lb) boned leg of lamb, trimmed and cut into 5 cm (2 inch) cubes*
- *350 g (12 oz) onion, peeled and roughly chopped*
- *4 garlic cloves, peeled and sliced*
- *2 red peppers, deseeded and roughly chopped*
- *700 g (1½ lb) potatoes, peeled and cut into large chunks*

560 CALS/SERVING

- *10 ml (2 tsp) ground ginger*
- *1 cinnamon stick, broken in two halves*
- *50 g (2 oz) pearl barley*
- *600 ml (1 pint) beef stock*
- *30 ml (2 tbsp) Worcestershire sauce*
- *salt and pepper*
- *lemon wedges and marjoram sprigs, to garnish*

1 Heat 45 ml (3 tbsp) oil in a large flameproof casserole and brown the meat in batches, adding a little more oil if necessary. Drain on absorbent kitchen paper.
2 Sauté onions and garlic until well browned. Add the peppers, potatoes, ginger, cinnamon and pearl barley; sauté for 2 minutes. Stir in the stock, Worcestershire sauce and plenty of seasoning. Bring to the boil and replace the meat.
3 Cover and cook at 170°C (325°F) mark 3 for about 2 hours or until the lamb is tender. Adjust the seasoning and garnish with lemon wedges and marjoram sprigs to serve.

3 Add the mustards, Worcestershire sauce and anchovy paste to the pan. Cook over moderate heat, stirring, for 1-2 minutes. Stir in the cream and bring to the boil. Return the kidneys and mushrooms to the pan. Stir to coat with the sauce and simmer for 5 minutes. Season to taste and transfer to a warm serving dish. Sprinkle with plenty of chopped parsley.

VARIATION Brown cap or oyster mushrooms are equally delicious with these kidneys as chanterelles.

GRILLED PORK WITH SPICED BUTTER

PREPARATION TIME 5 minutes
COOKING TIME 20 minutes
FREEZING Not suitable

SERVES 4
- *300 ml (10 fl oz) cider*
- *30 ml (2 tbsp) mixed peppercorns, crushed*
- *60 ml (4 tbsp) brown sugar*
- *60 ml (4 tbsp) wholegrain mustard*

455 CALS/SERVING
- *50 g (2 oz) butter*
- *salt and pepper*
- *4 pork chops, each weighing about 175 g (6 oz)*

1 Place the cider in a small saucepan and boil for 15 minutes.
2 Meanwhile, combine the peppercorns with the sugar, mustard and butter.
3 Season the chops and cook under a grill for 5 minutes on one side. Turn over, spread each chop with the butter, then cook for a further 5 minutes or until golden and cooked through.
4 Pour the grill pan juices into the cider and heat for 2-3 minutes. Pour over the pork chops and serve.

AUTUMN SPICED KIDNEYS

PREPARATION TIME 10 minutes
COOKING TIME About 20 minutes
FREEZING Not suitable

SERVES 4
- *50 g (2 oz) unsalted butter*
- *700 g (1½ lb) lamb's kidneys, skinned, halved and cored*
- *225 g (8 oz) chanterelle mushrooms, thickly sliced*
- *30 ml (2 tbsp) green peppercorn mustard (Maille)*
- *15 ml (1 tbsp) wholegrain mustard*

595 CALS/SERVING
- *dash of Worcestershire sauce*
- *5 ml (1 tsp) anchovy paste or essence*
- *300 ml (10 fl oz) double cream*
- *salt and pepper*
- *plenty of roughly chopped fresh parsley, to garnish*

1 Heat the butter in a frying pan until foaming. Add the kidneys in batches and cook briskly until brown. Remove from the pan with a slotted spoon and transfer to a sieve to drain out the bitter juices.
2 Fry the mushrooms in the same pan, stirring occasionally until just tender, and remove to the sieve.

BRAISED PORK CHOPS
WITH PLUMS AND GINGER

PREPARATION TIME 15 minutes
COOKING TIME About 50 minutes
FREEZING Suitable
❄

SERVES 4
- *450 g (1 lb) plums*
- *2.5 cm (1 inch) piece fresh root ginger, peeled and shredded*
- *salt and pepper*
- *15 g (½ oz) butter*
- *15 ml (1 tbsp) oil*
- *4 pork chops, each weighing about 200 g (7 oz)*

415 CALS/SERVING
- *60 ml (4 tbsp) white wine*
- *175 ml (6 fl oz) vegetable stock*
- *30 ml (2 tbsp) Greek yogurt*
- *30 ml (2 tbsp) chopped fresh tarragon*

1 Halve the plums, remove the stones, and cut into slices. Mix together with the ginger, then spread evenly over the base of a lightly greased ovenproof dish. Season with salt and pepper. Bake in the oven at 200°C (400°F) mark 6 for 15 minutes.

2 Heat the butter and oil in a frying pan, add the pork chops and fry on both sides until browned. Remove the pork with a slotted spoon and arrange on top of the plums.

3 Add the wine to the frying pan and cook briskly to reduce by half. Add the stock and cook for a further minute, scraping up any sediment from the bottom of the pan. Pour over the pork.

4 Return the dish of plums and pork to the oven and cook for a further 20-25 minutes until the pork is tender.

5 Transfer the chops to a warmed serving dish or plates. Stir the yogurt and tarragon into the plums, adjust the seasoning, then spoon the plums around the pork. Serve at once.

PORK LOIN STUFFED WITH FIGS

PREPARATION TIME 30 minutes
COOKING TIME 1¼ hours
FREEZING Not suitable

SERVES 4   630 CALS/SERVING

- *45 ml (3 tbsp) olive oil*
- *1 onion, peeled and finely chopped*
- *2 garlic cloves, peeled and chopped*
- *75 g (3 oz) breadcrumbs*
- *4 no-soak dried figs, finely chopped*
- *8 pitted green olives, finely chopped*
- *25 g (1 oz) flaked almonds, toasted and chopped*
- *15 ml (1 tbsp) lemon juice*
- *15 ml (1 tbsp) chopped fresh parsley*
- *1 egg yolk*
- *salt and pepper*
- *900 g (2 lb) boned loin of pork*
- *sprigs of flat-leaf parsley, to garnish*

1 Heat 30 ml (2 tbsp) oil in a frying pan, add the onion and garlic, and fry gently until soft. Stir in the next seven ingredients and season.
2 Remove the string from the pork and unroll the flap away from the fillet in the centre, cutting away any excess fat or meat if necessary. Spread about half the stuffing over the flat piece. Roll up, starting from the thick side. Tie at intervals with string.
3 Pour the remaining oil into a small roasting tin and add the pork. Roast at 200°C (400°F) mark 6 for about 1¼ hours.
4 Shape the remaining stuffing into walnut-sized balls and add to the roasting tin 15-20 minutes before the end of the cooking time.
5 Allow the meat to rest for 10 minutes before slicing. Serve garnished with parsley sprigs.

SPANISH PORK AND BEAN CASSEROLE

PREPARATION TIME 15 minutes, plus soaking
COOKING TIME 2¼ hours
FREEZING Not suitable

SERVES 6-8   620-465 CALS/SERVING

- *900 g (2 lb) shoulder of ham or gammon joint*
- *125 g (4 oz) dried haricot beans*
- *125 g (4 oz) dried butter beans*
- *15 ml (1 tbsp) olive oil*
- *50 g (2 oz) streaky bacon, rinded and cut into thin strips*
- *2 garlic cloves, peeled and crushed*
- *2 Spanish onions, peeled and sliced*
- *225 g (8 oz) leeks, washed, trimmed and sliced*
- *1 carrot, peeled and chopped*
- *1 bay leaf*
- *5 ml (1 tsp) paprika*
- *salt and pepper*
- *125 g (4 oz) chorizo or other spicy sausage, cut into 2.5 cm (1 inch) lengths*
- *125 g (4 oz) black pudding, sliced*
- *bay leaves, to garnish*

1 Soak the ham overnight in enough cold water to cover. In a separate bowl, soak the haricot beans and butter beans in enough cold water to cover.
2 Drain the soaked ham. Drain the soaked beans and rinse thoroughly under cold running water. Place the beans in a saucepan of water and boil rapidly for 10 minutes, then drain.
3 Heat the oil in a large flameproof casserole, add the bacon and cook gently for 2-3 minutes, then stir in the garlic, onions, leeks and carrot and continue cooking for 10 minutes.
4 Stir in the drained beans with the bay leaf and paprika. Cover with cold water and season with salt and pepper to taste. Bring to the boil, then lower the heat, cover and simmer for 30 minutes. Add the ham or gammon and simmer for a further hour.
5 Add the chorizo sausage and black pudding and simmer gently for a further 20-25 minutes.
6 Allow to cool slightly, then remove the ham with a slotted spoon. Remove the fat and any string from the ham, then cut into bite-sized pieces and return to the casserole. Discard the bay leaf. Reheat gently and serve hot, garnished with fresh bay leaves.

HARVEST PORK CASSEROLE

PREPARATION TIME 20 minutes
COOKING TIME 2 hours
FREEZING Suitable
❄

SERVES 4-6
- *45 ml (3 tbsp) oil*
- *700 g (1½ lb) boneless leg of pork, cut into pieces*
- *225 g (8 oz) onion, peeled and chopped*
- *1 garlic clove, peeled and crushed*
- *450 g (1 lb) parsnips, peeled and sliced*
- *15 ml (1 tbsp) ground coriander*
- *5 ml (1 tsp) cumin seeds or 15 ml (1 tbsp) ground cumin*

530-355 CALS/SERVING
- *30 ml (2 tbsp) white plain flour*
- *300 ml (10 fl oz) beef stock*
- *300 ml (10 fl oz) apple juice or cider*
- *salt and pepper*
- *2 small, crisp, red eating apples, roughly chopped*
- *snipped chives, to garnish*

1 Heat the oil in a flameproof casserole, add the meat and brown well. Remove with a slotted spoon and drain on absorbent kitchen paper.

2 Add the onion and garlic to the casserole and sauté for 2-3 minutes. Add the parsnips, coriander and cumin and sauté for 2 minutes. Stir in the flour. Off the heat, gradually add the stock, apple juice and seasoning.

3 Bring to the boil and replace the meat. Cover and cook at 170°C (325°F) mark 3 for 1¼ hours or until the pork is almost tender.

4 Stir the apple into the pork, cover and cook for a further 15-20 minutes or until tender. Season to taste and garnish with snipped chives.

NOTE Do not peel the apples, as the red skin adds colour and texture to the dish.

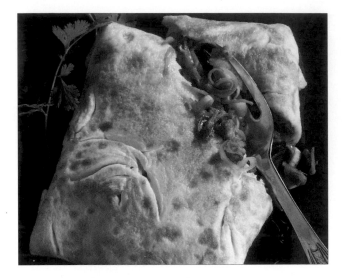

5 When the omelette is just set but still moist, tip the filling into the middle and fold the four sides over the top to encase, like a parcel. Invert a warmed plate over the wok or pan then turn out the filled omelette. Serve immediately.

VARIATIONS Substitute minced beef for the pork. For a vegetarian option, omit the meat altogether and replace with another vegetable, such as beansprouts.

STUFFED THAI OMELETTE

PREPARATION TIME 10 minutes
COOKING TIME About 15 minutes
FREEZING Not suitable
🕐

SERVES 2
- *3 eggs*
- *salt and pepper*
- *45 ml (3 tbsp) vegetable oil*
- *125 g (4 oz) minced pork*
- *1 large garlic clove, peeled and crushed*
- *2.5 cm (1 inch) piece fresh root ginger, peeled and grated*
- *1 carrot, peeled and grated*
- *1 small leek, trimmed and shredded*

460 CALS/SERVING
- *1 tomato, skinned and finely chopped*
- *5 ml (1 tsp) soft brown sugar*
- *15 ml (1 tbsp) nam pla (Thai fish sauce) (optional)*
- *10-15 ml (2-3 tsp) soy sauce*
- *5-15 ml (1-3 tsp) rice vinegar or cider vinegar*

1 In a bowl, beat the eggs together lightly, and season with salt and pepper.
2 Heat half of the oil in a wok or frying pan. Add the pork with the garlic and ginger and stir-fry until the pork is cooked through.
3 Add the carrot and leek and stir-fry for 1 minute, then add the tomato, sugar, fish sauce if using, soy sauce and vinegar. Season generously with pepper and stir-fry for 2-3 minutes. Transfer to a warmed dish and keep warm.
4 Wipe out the wok or frying pan, place over a moderate heat and add the remaining oil; swirl to distribute evenly. Pour in the beaten eggs.

CARAMELIZED ONION AND GRUYERE FRITTATA

PREPARATION TIME 10 minutes
COOKING TIME 40 minutes
FREEZING Not suitable
♡

SERVES 4
- *30 ml (2 tbsp) vegetable oil*
- *700 g (1½ lb) onions, peeled and sliced*
- *1 garlic clove, peeled and sliced*
- *4 eggs*
- *15 ml (1 tbsp) each chopped fresh chives and parsley*

330 CALS/SERVING
- *salt and pepper*
- *125 g (4 oz) fresh spinach, roughly chopped*
- *75 g (3 oz) each Gruyère and Edam cheese, cut into 1 cm (½ inch) cubes*

1 Heat the oil in a small 9 cm (7½ inch) non-stick frying pan. Cook the onions and the garlic, covered, for 25-30 minutes or until caramelized and golden brown, stirring occasionally.
2 Beat together the eggs and herbs with plenty of seasoning.
3 Remove the onions from the pan and add the spinach. Stir over a low heat until wilted and all the excess moisture has evaporated. Return the onions to the pan with the cheese and stir until the mixture is thoroughly combined.
4 Pour in the egg mixture and allow to run through the onions. Cook over a medium heat, loosening the edge with a spatula, for about 3-4 minutes or until the base and edge of the mixture are set. Cover the pan handle with foil and place under a hot grill for a further 3-4 minutes or until the top is set and golden brown.

POACHED EGGS ON TOASTED BACON BAGUETTE

PREPARATION TIME 10 minutes
COOKING TIME 20 minutes
FREEZING Not suitable

SERVES 4

- *450 g (1 lb) cherry tomatoes, halved*
- *2 garlic cloves, peeled and crushed*
- *black pepper*
- *1 baguette*
- *60 ml (4 tbsp) mayonnaise*
- *15 ml (1 tbsp) olive oil*

520 CALS/SERVING

- *300 g (10 oz) thinly cut rindless streaky bacon*
- *30 ml (2 tbsp) chopped fresh parsley*
- *4 eggs*
- *1 small frisée lettuce*

1 Put the tomatoes in a bowl. Stir in the garlic and season well with black pepper.

2 Cut the bread into four lengths and slice each piece in half but not all the way through. Spread the inside of each piece with 15 ml (1 tbsp) mayonnaise, then toast the inside under a hot grill. Keep warm, covered, under a low grill.

3 Heat the oil in a non-stick frying pan and fry the bacon in two batches until crispy and golden brown. Keep warm. Quickly fry the tomatoes in the bacon fat for about 1 minute and stir in the parsley.

4 Lightly poach the eggs in an egg poacher or deep frying pan.

5 Top the baguette pieces with frisée, bacon, warm tomatoes and an egg. Grind over pepper to serve.

TIP
To poach eggs in a frying pan, fill to a depth of 7.5 cm (3 inches) with water, adding 30 ml (2 tbsp) vinegar. Bring to the boil, swirl the water, then slip the eggs in. Cook gently for about 4 minutes until lightly set.

CHICK-PEA AND PARSNIP SOUFFLES

PREPARATION TIME 20 minutes
COOKING TIME 2 hours
FREEZING Not suitable
♡

SERVES 4

- *175 g (6 oz) chick-peas, soaked overnight and drained*
- *450 g (1 lb) parsnips, peeled and cut into chunks*
- *salt and pepper*
- *50 g (2 oz) margarine*
- *45 ml (3 tbsp) white plain flour*

165 CALS/SERVING

- *300 ml (10 fl oz) semi-skimmed milk*
- *3 eggs, separated*
- *10 ml (2 tsp) mild curry powder*
- *50 g (2 oz) freshly grated Parmesan cheese*
- *fresh salad leaves, to garnish (optional)*

1 Boil the chick-peas in water to cover for 10 minutes, then drain and cover again with fresh water. Bring to the boil and simmer for 1½ hours or until tender, then drain.
2 Meanwhile, cook the parsnips in a saucepan of boiling salted water until just tender. Drain.
3 Melt the margarine in a saucepan, stir in the flour and cook, stirring, for 1-2 minutes. Gradually stir in the milk off the heat, then bring to the boil, stirring, and simmer for 2-3 minutes. Remove from the heat, cool slightly, then stir in the egg yolks, salt and pepper, curry powder and all but 45 ml (3 tbsp) of the cheese.
4 Purée the parsnips, chick-peas and sauce mixture together in a blender or food processor until almost smooth. Transfer to a bowl. Season.
5 Grease four deep 450 ml (15 fl oz) ovenproof dishes and coat with a little of the remaining cheese.
6 Whisk the egg whites until stiff but not dry, then fold into the mixture. Spoon into the prepared dishes and sprinkle over the remaining cheese.
7 Bake in the oven at 200°C (400°F) mark 6 for about 20 minutes or until the soufflés are well risen, golden brown and just set. Serve immediately, garnished with fresh salad leaves.

NOTE These delicious individual soufflés make a tasty starter or light lunch dish.

MELTING CHEESE AND HAM PARCEL

PREPARATION TIME 15 minutes, plus chilling
COOKING TIME 25 minutes
FREEZING Not suitable

SERVES 4

- *45 ml (3 tbsp) crème fraîche*
- *15 ml (1 tbsp) Dijon mustard*
- *370 g (13 oz) packet puff pastry*
- *350 g (12 oz) good-quality cooked ham, sliced*

685 CALS/SERVING

- *175 g (6 oz) Gruyère cheese, thinly sliced or grated*
- *1 egg yolk, beaten*
- *sea salt*

1 Mix together the crème fraîche and Dijon mustard.
2 Roll out a third of the puff pastry into a rectangle measuring 30 x 25 cm (12 x 10 inches) and place on a baking sheet.
3 Spread a third of the mustard mixture evenly over the pastry, leaving a 1 cm (½ inch) border. Top with a layer of ham, half the remaining mustard mixture, all the cheese and the remaining ham.
4 Spread the remaining mustard mixture over the ham and brush the pastry border with beaten egg yolk.
5 Roll out the remaining pastry into a rectangle about 2.5 cm (1 inch) larger than the base. Place the pastry over the filling and press the edges firmly together. Trim if necessary. Knock the edges up with a knife. Brush with beaten egg yolk and chill for 15 minutes.
6 Cook the parcel at 220°C (425°F) mark 7 for 25 minutes or until golden brown and the pastry base is cooked. If the pastry begins to burn around the edges, cover with foil and return to the oven to finish cooking. Season with sea salt.

NOTE Make sure the oven is preheated before cooking the parcel, otherwise the pastry could be disappointingly soggy.

AUBERGINE AND PEPPER
PARMIGIANA

PREPARATION TIME 15 minutes
COOKING TIME 1¼ hours
FREEZING Suitable (stage 4)
✻

SERVES 6

- *two 400 g (14 oz) cans chopped tomatoes*
- *30 ml (2 tbsp) olive oil*
- *2 garlic cloves, peeled and crushed*
- *30 ml (2 tbsp) chopped fresh basil*
- *5 ml (1 tsp) grated lemon rind*
- *pinch of sugar*

360 CALS/SERVING

- *salt and pepper*
- *4 large red peppers, deseeded and quartered*
- *3 aubergines*
- *225 g (8 oz) Cheddar cheese, grated*
- *50 g (2 oz) freshly grated Parmesan cheese*

1 Start by making the tomato sauce. Place the chopped tomatoes in a saucepan and add half the oil, the garlic, basil, lemon rind, sugar and seasoning. Bring to the boil, cover and simmer gently for 30 minutes. Remove the lid and cook for a further 15 minutes. Allow to cool.

2 Meanwhile, place the pepper quarters on the grill pan, brush with a little oil and grill for 5-6 minutes on each side until charred and tender. Transfer to a plastic bag and leave to cool.

3 Cut the aubergines lengthways into thick slices, place on the grill pan and brush with oil. Grill for 6-8 minutes on each side, then leave to cool. Peel the cooled peppers.

4 Spoon a little sauce into the base of a large greased dish and top with a layer of aubergines and peppers. Sprinkle over a little of the Cheddar cheese. Continue to add layers of sauce, vegetables and cheese, finishing with a layer of Cheddar cheese. Sprinkle over the Parmesan.

5 Bake in the oven at 200°C (400°F) mark 6 for 30-40 minutes until bubbling and golden. Serve at once.

NOODLES WITH MEATBALLS AND SHALLOTS

PREPARATION TIME 25 minutes
COOKING TIME 15 minutes
FREEZING Not suitable
♡

SERVES 4   335 CALS/SERVING
- *300 g (10 oz) shallots, peeled*
- *30 ml (2 tbsp) olive oil*
- *225 g (8 oz) lean minced beef*
- *30 ml (2 tbsp) chopped fresh parsley*
- *salt and pepper*
- *25 g (1 oz) pitted black olives*
- *30 ml (2 tbsp) chopped chives*
- *30 ml (2 tbsp) pesto sauce*
- *125 g (4 oz) dried noodles*

1 Chop 50 g (2 oz) shallots and sauté in 15 ml (1 tbsp) oil until golden. Cool, then mix with the beef mince, parsley and seasoning. Shape into 8 small patties. Fry in a non-stick pan for about 5-7 minutes each side or until cooked through.
2 Meanwhile, thinly slice the remaining shallots. Cook in the remaining oil in a covered pan for about 8-10 minutes until golden. Stir in the olives, chives and pesto, warm through and season.
3 Cook the noodles in boiling salted water until just tender, then drain well.
4 Toss the noodles with the shallot mixture and serve immediately accompanied by the meatballs.

SEAFOOD SPAGHETTI WITH PEPPER AND ALMOND SAUCE

PREPARATION TIME 20 minutes
COOKING TIME 20 minutes
FREEZING Not suitable
♡

SERVES 4   305 CALS/SERVING
- *1 small red pepper, about 150 g (5 oz)*
- *1 fresh red chilli*
- *50 g (2 oz) toasted, blanched almonds*
- *2-3 garlic cloves, peeled and crushed*
- *30 ml (2 tbsp) red wine vinegar*
- *350 ml (12 fl oz) tomato juice*
- *60 ml (4 tbsp) chopped fresh parsley*
- *salt and pepper*
- *125 g (4 oz) dried spaghetti*
- *450 g (1 lb) cooked mixed seafood, such as prawns, mussels and squid*
- *chopped fresh chilli, to garnish*

1 Place the pepper and chilli under the grill and cook, turning occasionally, until the skins char and blacken. Cool slightly, then pull off the skins. Halve, discard the seeds, then put the flesh into a large food processor bowl.
2 Add the nuts, garlic, vinegar, tomato juice, half the parsley and seasoning. Blend until almost smooth. Transfer to a pan.
3 Cook the pasta in boiling salted water until just tender (*al dente*). Drain and toss in the rest of the fresh parsley. Season to taste and cover.
4 Meanwhile, gently heat the sauce until it simmers, then add the seafood. Simmer for 3-5 minutes or until heated through, stirring frequently. Adjust the seasoning and serve immediately over the spaghetti. Garnish with chopped fresh chilli.

> *TIPS*
> Remember to wear rubber gloves when handling chillies to prevent skin irritation. You can buy fresh or frozen mixed cooked seafood in supermarkets. If you can't find it, put together your own selection of prepared cooked seafood.

PASTITSIO

PREPARATION TIME 10 minutes, plus cooling
COOKING TIME 2 hours
FREEZING Suitable (stage 3)

❊

SERVES 4

- *45 ml (3 tbsp) olive oil*
- *125 g (4 oz) onion, peeled and finely chopped*
- *2 garlic cloves, peeled and crushed*
- *450 g (1 lb) lean minced lamb*
- *7.5 ml (1½ tsp) dried oregano*
- *5 ml (1 tsp) each dried thyme, ground cinnamon, ground cumin*
- *2.5 ml (½ tsp) each ground ginger and grated nutmeg*
- *1 bay leaf*

675 CALS/SERVING

- *150 ml (5 fl oz) dry white wine*
- *400 g (14 oz) can chopped tomatoes*
- *salt and pepper*
- *125 g (4 oz) pasta, such as macaroni*
- *45 ml (3 tbsp) chopped fresh coriander (optional)*
- *25 g (1 oz) butter*
- *25 g (1 oz) white plain flour*
- *450 ml (15 fl oz) milk*
- *50 g (2 oz) freshly grated Parmesan cheese*
- *2 eggs, beaten*

1 Heat the oil in a saucepan, add the onion and garlic and cook gently for about 10 minutes, stirring occasionally, until the onions are soft.
2 Add the lamb. Cook over a high heat for about 5 minutes, stirring, until evenly browned. Stir in the herbs, spices and bay leaf. Cook over a moderate heat for a further 5 minutes, stirring occasionally.
3 Mix in the wine, tomatoes and seasoning. Bring to the boil, lower the heat and simmer, covered, for 30 minutes. Uncover and cook for about 15 minutes, stirring occasionally, until the sauce is thickened and well reduced. Adjust the seasoning. Cool and skim off all the fat.
4 Cook the pasta in boiling, salted water until just tender (*al dente*). Drain. Stir into the lamb with the chopped coriander, if using. Spoon into a shallow ovenproof dish.
5 Melt the butter in a saucepan. Stir in the flour, seasoning and milk. Bring to the boil, stirring, then simmer for 3-4 minutes or until thickened. Cool slightly. Off the heat, beat in the Parmesan cheese and eggs. Pour over the lamb mixture.
6 Cook at 190°C (375°F) mark 5 for 35-40 minutes or until golden brown and piping hot. Serve at once with a green salad.

JAPANESE NOODLES WITH PAK CHOI AND MOOLI

PREPARATION TIME 15 minutes
COOKING TIME 30 minutes
FREEZING Not suitable
♡

SERVES 4

- *125 g (4 oz) flat rice or egg noodles*
- *30 ml (2 tbsp) sunflower oil*
- *1 garlic clove, peeled and sliced*
- *5 ml (1 tsp) freshly grated root ginger*
- *pinch of sugar*
- *3 pak choi, about 350 g (12 oz) total weight, roughly chopped*
- *1.1 litres (2 pints) vegetable stock*

215 CALS/SERVING

- *30 ml (2 tbsp) miso*
- *15 ml (1 tbsp) lemon juice*
- *15 ml (1 tbsp) light soy sauce*
- *125 g (4 oz) mooli, sliced*
- *1 packet mustard and cress, cut*
- *15 ml (1 tbsp) chopped fresh coriander*

1 Cook the noodles according to the packet instructions. Drain, refresh under cold water and drain again. Set aside.
2 Heat the oil in a saucepan and fry the garlic, ginger and sugar over a low heat for 2 minutes. Add the pak choi, in a single layer if possible, cover and cook over a low heat for 5 minutes. Add the stock, miso, lemon juice, soy sauce and mooli, bring to the boil, cover and simmer for 15 minutes.
3 Stir in the noodles, mustard and cress and coriander. Heat through for 1 minute and serve at once.

NOTE Miso is a thick paste made from fermented soya beans and is fermented together with either barley or rice. It is used to flavour soups, sauces, stews etc. Miso is available from good health food stores.

VARIATION Use another Chinese cabbage in place of pak choi. Mooli (related to the radish) is a popular Japanese ingredient and gives this dish a distinctive oriental flavour, but if it is unavailable use thinly sliced turnip instead.

PUMPKIN RAVIOLI WITH HERBS

PREPARATION TIME About 45 minutes
COOKING TIME 1¼ hours
FREEZING Suitable (stage 4)
❋

SERVES 4

490 CALS/SERVING

- *200 g (7 oz) '00' pasta flour*
- *2 eggs (size 3)*
FILLING
- *450 g (1 lb) wedge pumpkin*
- *30 ml (2 tbsp) olive oil*
- *75 g (3 oz) prosciutto or Parma ham, finely chopped*
- *50 g (2 oz) Parmesan cheese, finely grated*

- *20 ml (1½ tbsp) chopped fresh basil*
- *20 ml (1½ tbsp) chopped fresh parsley*
- *1 egg yolk*
- *freshly grated nutmeg, to taste*
- *30 ml (2 tbsp) double cream*
- *salt and pepper*
- *melted butter and chopped fresh herbs, to serve*

1 Brush the pumpkin flesh with the oil and bake in the oven at 190°C (375°F) mark 5 for about 1 hour until soft. Scrape out the flesh and mash until smooth. Add all the other filling ingredients.
2 To make the pasta, heap the flour on a work surface and make a well in the centre. Break the eggs into the well and work the flour into the eggs with your fingers to form a dough. Knead lightly for about 5 minutes. Wrap in clingfilm and leave to rest for 15 minutes.
3 Roll out the pasta dough as thinly as possible on an unfloured surface. Keep covered with clingfilm to prevent drying out.
4 Take a strip of pasta 10-12 cm (4-5 inches) wide. Spoon on heaped teaspoonfuls of stuffing at 6 cm (2½ inch) intervals. Brush the edges and between the stuffing with a little water. Cover with another sheet of pasta and press along the edges and between the stuffing to seal. Cut between the stuffing at 6 cm (2½ inch) intervals and cut neatly along the long edges. Repeat to use all of the pasta and stuffing, to make 20-24 ravioli.
5 Cook the ravioli in batches in boiling water for about 3 minutes until the sealed edges are just tender (*al dente*). Drain and serve tossed in melted butter and chopped herbs.

CALABRIAN PASTA

PREPARATION TIME 10 minutes
COOKING TIME 12-15 minutes
FREEZING Not suitable
🕐

SERVES 4-6

695-465 CALS/SERVING

- *50 g (2 oz) sultanas*
- *150 g (5 oz) broccoli, cut into small florets*
- *300-350 g (10-12 oz) long fusilli or spaghetti*
- *salt and pepper*
- *125 ml (4 fl oz) olive oil*
- *75 g (3 oz) white breadcrumbs*

- *2 garlic cloves, peeled and finely chopped*
- *25 g (1 oz) pine nuts*
- *10 ml (2 tsp) anchovy essence or anchovy paste*
- *45 ml (3 tbsp) chopped fresh parsley*
- *cayenne pepper, to taste*

1 Bring about 600 ml (1 pint) water to the boil. Put the sultanas in a bowl, pour on a little of the boiling water and leave to soak. Pour the rest of the boiling water over the broccoli in a pan and simmer for 30 seconds; drain.
2 Cook the pasta in a large pan of boiling salted water until just tender (*al dente*).
3 Meanwhile, heat the oil in a frying pan and add the breadcrumbs. Fry, stirring, until they begin to crisp, then add the garlic and pine nuts. Continue to fry, stirring until the pine nuts begin to colour, then add the broccoli to heat through.
4 Drain the pasta, setting it back on top of the saucepan to catch the last 15 ml (1 tbsp) cooking water. Stir the anchovy essence or paste and drained sultanas into this liquid, then return the pasta to the pan. Toss with a generous grinding of black pepper and half of the chopped parsley. Transfer to a heated serving bowl.
5 Mix the remaining parsley into the crumb mixture and sprinkle over the pasta. Sprinkle with cayenne pepper and toss at the table.

TIP
It's an Italian trick to toss the pasta with a little of its cooking water. This helps to keep the pasta hot, as well as preventing it from drying out before serving.

BAKED VEGETABLES WITH A SPICY SAUCE

PREPARATION TIME 30 minutes, plus standing
COOKING TIME 40 minutes
FREEZING Not suitable

SERVES 4-6　　　　　**425-285 CALS/SERVING**

- 6-8 *cherry tomatoes*
- 2-3 *rosemary sprigs*
- 125 ml (4 fl oz) *extra-virgin olive oil*
- *coarse sea salt and pepper*
- 1 *red and 1 yellow or orange pepper, deseeded and halved*
- 6 *shallots, peeled*
- 1 *aubergine, cut into thin slices*
- 2-3 *courgettes, thickly sliced on the diagonal*
- 1 *fennel bulb, quartered lengthwise*
- 175 g (6 oz) *parsnips, halved*
- 125 g (4 oz) *baby sweetcorn, halved lengthwise*

- 225 g (8 oz) *mushrooms (large closed cup), left whole*

SPICY SAUCE
- 15 ml (1 tbsp) *sunflower oil*
- 1 *small onion, peeled and finely sliced*
- 1 *garlic clove, peeled and finely sliced*
- 1 *green chilli, deseeded and finely sliced*
- 10 ml (2 tsp) *capers*
- 10 ml (2 tsp) *soft brown sugar*
- *juice of ½ lemon*
- 175 g (6 oz) *passata*

1 Cut a shallow cross in the base of each tomato, but leave them whole. Strip the leaves from one of the rosemary sprigs and chop finely. Pour the olive oil into a large bowl and add the chopped rosemary and whole sprigs with salt and pepper. Add the vegetables and turn to coat evenly with the oil. Leave to infuse for at least 1-2 hours.
2 Put all the vegetables, except the cherry tomatoes, into a large shallow baking tin with the rosemary sprigs and baste with the oil. Bake at 220°C (425°F) mark 7, turning and basting from time to time, for about 40 minutes until the vegetables are evenly browned and cooked through. Add the cherry tomatoes 10 minutes before the end of the cooking time.
3 To make the sauce, heat the oil in a small pan, add the onion, garlic and chilli and fry gently until tender.
4 Meanwhile put the capers, sugar, lemon juice and passata in a blender or food processor and work until smooth. Season with salt and pepper

and add to the chilli mixture. Cover and cook for 5-10 minutes, stirring occasionally, to make a thick sauce.
5 Transfer the baked vegetables to an oval serving platter and serve at once, accompanied by the sauce.

QUICK TOMATO AND GARLIC PIZZA

PREPARATION TIME 15 minutes
COOKING TIME 20 minutes
FREEZING Not suitable
🕑

SERVES 2　　　　　**485 CALS/SERVING**

- 1 *garlic bulb*
- *olive oil, for basting*
- 4 *tomatoes, about 400 g (14 oz) total weight, roughly chopped*
- *salt and pepper*
- 145 g (5.1 oz) *packet pizza-base mix*

- 15 ml (1 tbsp) *chopped fresh rosemary or 10 ml (2 tsp) dried*
- 75 g (3 oz) *feta cheese*
- *about 8 black olives*
- *about 8 fresh basil leaves*

1 Divide the garlic into cloves, discarding the outer, papery layers, but leaving the inner skins intact. Toss in a little oil. Put the tomatoes in a bowl with 5 ml (1 tsp) salt. Mix well.
2 Make up the pizza base mix according to the packet instructions. As you are kneading the dough, knead in the rosemary until it is evenly incorporated.
3 Roll out the dough thinly to a 25 cm (10 inch) round on a lightly floured surface. Transfer to a lightly greased and floured baking sheet.
4 Spoon the tomatoes over the pizza base to within 1 cm (½ inch) of the edge and crumble the feta cheese on top. Scatter the olives, garlic cloves and basil over the top. Season with pepper only.
5 Bake in the oven at 220°C (425°F) mark 7 for 20 minutes or until the base is crisp and golden. Serve, mashing the garlic as you eat.

VARIATION Replace the garlic, olives and feta cheese with a 350 g (12 oz) jar of pimientos, drained; 20 ml (4 tsp) capers; and 75 g (3 oz) smoked vegetarian cheese.

VEGETABLE CHEESE PIE WITH POTATO CRUST

PREPARATION TIME 55 minutes, plus cooling
COOKING TIME 1 hour 10 minutes
FREEZING Suitable
❄

SERVES 4
- *225 g (8 oz) white plain flour*
- *salt and pepper*
- *100 g (3½ oz) butter, diced*
- *175 g (6 oz) mashed potato*

FILLING
- *25 g (1 oz) butter*
- *2 large onions, peeled and sliced*
- *4 garlic cloves, peeled and crushed*
- *350 g (12 oz) celeriac, peeled and cut into chunks*
- *50 g (2 oz) white plain flour*
- *300 ml (10 fl oz) vegetable stock*

645 CALS/SERVING
- *300 ml (10 fl oz) milk*
- *175 g (6 oz) broccoli, cut into small florets*
- *125 g (4 oz) French beans, trimmed and cut into 2.5 cm (1 inch) lengths*
- *2 large carrots, peeled and cut into chunks*
- *grated nutmeg*
- *400 g (14 oz) can pinto or red kidney beans, drained*
- *225 g (8 oz) Cheddar cheese, grated*
- *egg yolk, to glaze*

1 To make the pastry, sift the flour and salt into a bowl. Add the butter, and rub in with the fingertips. Add the mashed potato and about 20-25 ml (4-5 tsp) cold water. Mix to a firm dough and knead lightly. Chill while making the filling.
2 To make the filling, melt the butter in a large saucepan. Add the onions and garlic and fry gently for 5 minutes. Add the celeriac and fry for a further 10 minutes. Stir in the flour and cook for 1 minute. Gradually stir in the stock and milk and bring just to the boil, stirring.
3 Add the broccoli, French beans and carrots. Season with nutmeg and salt and pepper. Cover and cook gently for 15 minutes. Cool slightly, then stir in the canned beans and cheese. Turn the filling into a pie dish.
4 Roll out the pastry on a lightly floured surface until 5 cm (2 inches) larger than the diameter of the dish. Cut off a 2.5 cm (1 inch) strip of pastry from around the edges.
5 Moisten the rim of the pie dish with water and position the strip on the rim. Dampen the pastry strip and position the pastry lid, pressing the edges firmly together to seal. Flute the edge and make a hole in the top of the pie to allow the steam to escape. If wished, decorate with pastry trimmings.
6 Brush the pie with beaten egg to glaze and sprinkle with a little nutmeg. Bake at 200°C (400°F) mark 6 for 30-35 minutes until the pastry is golden.

and the mixture is quite dry (about 15 minutes). Add the drained wild mushrooms and cook for a further 5 minutes. Remove from the heat and set aside. Season.

4 Stir the nuts, wild rice and apricots into the mushroom mixture.

5 Butter one sheet of filo pastry with a little melted butter, fold in half and butter again – you should have a piece about 23 cm (9 inches) square. Place one-sixth of the mushroom mixture in the middle and gather up the sides to form a parcel. Press gently to seal. Continue with the remaining pastry and mushroom mixture. Brush with melted butter and sprinkle with sesame seeds.

6 Place the parcels on a heated baking sheet and cook at 190°C (375°F) mark 5 for 25-30 minutes.

7 Stir the chives into the crème fraîche; season. Arrange the parcels on plates with a spoonful of the sauce. Garnish with chives. Serve the remaining sauce separately.

MIXED MUSHROOM PARCELS

PREPARATION TIME 45 minutes
COOKING TIME 1¼ hours
FREEZING Not suitable

SERVES 6
- 50 g (2 oz) wild or brown rice
- salt and pepper
- about 125 g (4 oz) butter
- 175 g (6 oz) onion, chopped
- 2 garlic cloves, peeled and crushed
- 175 g (6 oz) celery, chopped
- 175 g (6 oz) carrot, peeled and chopped
- 700 g (1½ lb) brown- and white-cap mushrooms, chopped

450 CALS/SERVING
- 225 g (8 oz) jar mixed wild mushrooms in oil
- 75 g (3 oz) toasted hazelnuts, chopped
- 75 g (3 oz) no-soak dried apricots, chopped
- 6 sheets filo pastry
- 15 ml (1 tbsp) sesame seeds
- 60 ml (4 tbsp) chopped fresh chives
- 200 g (7 oz) crème fraîche
- snipped chives, to garnish

1 Cook the rice in plenty of boiling salted water until tender. Drain and set aside.

2 Melt 25 g (1 oz) butter in a large frying pan and cook the onion and crushed garlic for about 10 minutes or until soft and brown. Add the celery and carrot and fry for 3-4 minutes.

3 Add a further 25 g (1 oz) butter and the fresh mushrooms to the vegetables. Cook uncovered, stirring, until all excess moisture has evaporated

GNOCCHI WITH RED PESTO

PREPARATION TIME 30 minutes
COOKING TIME 30-40 minutes,
FREEZING Not suitable

SERVES 4-6
- 900 g (2 lb) floury potatoes
- salt
- 50 g (2 oz) butter
- 1 egg beaten
- 225-275 g (8-10 oz) white plain flour
- basil leaves, to garnish
PESTO
- 1 large red pepper
- 50 g (2 oz) fresh basil
- 1 garlic clove, peeled and crushed

980-655 CALS/SERVING
- 30 ml (2 tbsp) toasted pine nuts
- 6 sun-dried tomatoes in oil, drained
- 2 ripe tomatoes, skinned
- 45 ml (3 tbsp) tomato purée
- 2.5 ml (½ tsp) chilli powder
- 50 g (2 oz) freshly grated Parmesan
- 150 ml (5 fl oz) olive oil

1 To make the pesto, grill the pepper, turning occasionally, until blackened all over. Cool, then peel off the skin. Remove the core and seeds. Place in a blender or food processor with all the remaining pesto ingredients, except the oil. Blend until smooth, then, with the machine running, slowly add the oil.

2 To make the gnocchi, cook the unpeeled potatoes in boiling water for 20-30 minutes until very tender. Drain well, then halve and press through a potato ricer, or peel and press through a sieve into a bowl.

3 While the potato is still warm, add 5 ml (1 tsp) salt, the butter, beaten egg and half the flour. Lightly mix together, then turn out onto a floured board. Gradually knead in enough remaining flour to yield a soft, slightly sticky dough.

4 Roll the dough into thick sausages, 2.5 cm (1 inch) in diameter. Cut into 2 cm (¾ inch) pieces. Roll each piece over the back of a fork with your floured thumb to form ridges on one side and an indentation on the other. Lay on a floured tea towel.

5 Bring a large saucepan of salted water to the boil. Cook the gnocchi in batches. Drop them into the boiling water and cook for 2-3 minutes, until they float to the surface. Remove with a slotted spoon and keep hot while cooking the remainder. Toss with the red pesto and garnish with basil.

FILLED BAKED POTATOES

PREPARATION TIME 15 minutes
COOKING TIME 1-1½ hours
FREEZING Not suitable

SERVES 8

- *8 large potatoes, each weighing about 175 g (6 oz)*

CARROT, PEANUT AND ALFALFA FILLING

- *75 ml (5 tbsp) natural yogurt*
- *45 ml (3 tbsp) peanut butter*
- *45 ml (3 tbsp) mayonnaise*
- *4 large carrots, peeled and coarsely grated*
- *75 g (3 oz) roasted peanuts*
- *75 g (3 oz) alfalfa sprouts*
- *a squeeze of lemon juice*
- *black pepper*

335 CALS/SERVING

HOT CHILLI BEAN FILLING

- *400 g (14 oz) can chopped tomatoes*
- *10 ml (2 tsp) tomato purée*
- *2 garlic cloves, peeled and crushed*
- *2.5 ml (½ tsp) chilli powder*
- *2.5 ml (½ tsp) dried oregano*
- *425 g (15 oz) cooked red kidney beans or 400 g (14 oz) can red kidney beans, drained and rinsed*
- *30 ml (2 tbsp) chopped fresh coriander or parsley*
- *salt and pepper*

1 Wash and scrub the potatoes and prick all over with a fork.

2 Bake the potatoes in the oven at 230°C (450°F) mark 8 for about 1 hour or at 200°C (400°F) mark 6 for about 1½ hours or until the potatoes feel soft when gently squeezed, turning them over once during cooking.

3 Meanwhile, make the fillings. For the Carrot, Peanut and Alfalfa filling, beat the yogurt, peanut butter and mayonnaise together, then gradually fold in the carrots, peanuts and alfalfa. Season with lemon juice and black pepper.

4 For the Hot Chilli Bean filling, put all the ingredients into a saucepan, season with salt and pepper, and bring to the boil. Cook vigorously for 15-20 minutes or until reduced and thickened.

5 When the potatoes are cooked, cut them in half and mash the flesh lightly with a fork. Top eight potato halves with one filling and the remaining potato halves with the second filling.

VARIATION Keep the potatoes whole and offer one or other of the fillings.

MARROW WITH TOMATO AND ONION

PREPARATION TIME 20 minutes
COOKING TIME 30 minutes
FREEZING Not suitable
♡

SERVES 4-6   100-65 CALS/SERVING
- *1 marrow*
- *25 g (1 oz) butter or margarine*
- *2 onions, peeled and chopped*
- *1 garlic clove, peeled and crushed*
- *6 large tomatoes, skinned and chopped*

- *30 ml (2 tbsp) tomato purée*
- *30 ml (2 tbsp) chopped mixed herbs or 10 ml (2 tsp) dried*
- *salt and pepper*
- *parsley sprigs, to garnish*

1 Peel the marrow, cut in half lengthways and scoop out the seeds. Cut the flesh into 2.5 cm (1 inch) cubes.
2 Melt the butter in a large saucepan and gently fry the onions and garlic for 5 minutes, until soft. Add the marrow and cook for a further 5 minutes.
3 Stir in the tomatoes, tomato purée and herbs. Cover and simmer for 20 minutes, until the vegetables are tender. Season to taste. Serve at once, garnished with parsley.

MIXED ONION CASSEROLE WITH JUNIPER

PREPARATION TIME 15 minutes
COOKING TIME 1¾ hours
FREEZING Not suitable

SERVES 4   460 CALS/SERVING
- *6 onions*
- *1 bunch of spring onions*
- *8 juniper berries*
- *50 g (2 oz) butter*
- *5 garlic cloves, peeled and finely sliced*
- *approximately 600 ml (1 pint) vegetable stock*
- *coarse sea salt and pepper*

- *6-8 shallots, peeled*
- *6 slices French bread, 1 cm (½ inch) thick*
- *125 g (4 oz) coarsely grated vegetarian mature Cheddar cheese*
- *15 ml (1 tbsp) snipped chives, to garnish*

1 Peel four of the onions, taking care to trim the minimum from the tops and bases. Cut each one crosswise into quarters, leaving the root end intact to ensure the onions do not fall apart during cooking.
2 Peel, halve and slice the remaining two ordinary onions. Trim the spring onions, then slice both the white and green parts. Crush the juniper berries, using a pestle and mortar.
3 Melt the butter in a saucepan, add the sliced ordinary onions, garlic and juniper berries and fry gently until golden. Add 300 ml (10 fl oz) of the vegetable stock and bring to the boil. Season with salt and pepper.
4 Stand the quarter-cut onions upright in a 1.2 litre (2 pint) casserole and add the shallots and sliced spring onions. Spoon the sautéed onion and garlic mixture on top. Cook, uncovered, in the oven at 180°C (350°F) mark 4 for 1½ hours, checking occasionally that the liquid hasn't dried out. Top up with more stock as necessary. At the end of the cooking time the liquid should be thick and syrupy.
5 About 15 minutes before the end of the cooking time, butter the slices of French bread and arrange butter-side up on top of the onion mixture. Sprinkle with the grated cheese and return to the oven to crisp and brown. (If, by the end of the cooking time, the cheese has not browned, flash the dish under a hot grill for 1-2 minutes until the

cheese is bubbling.) Sprinkle with the snipped chives to garnish and serve immediately, directly from the casserole.

NOTE The temperature isn't crucial for this dish, so if you are cooking a main course at a higher temperature, simply position the casserole lower in the oven.

SPICED PUMPKIN FRITTERS

PREPARATION TIME 15 minutes
COOKING TIME About 15 minutes
FREEZING Not suitable

🕐

SERVES 4
- *700 g (1½ lb) pumpkin flesh, deseeded*
- *175 g (6 oz) wholemeal plain flour*
- *2.5-5 ml (½-1 tsp) salt*
- *1.25 ml (¼ tsp) baking powder*
- *5 ml (1 tsp) cumin seeds*
- *2.5 ml (½ tsp) ground cumin*
- *1 egg, separated*

355 CALS/SERVING
- *1 small onion, peeled and finely chopped*
- *1-2 garlic cloves, peeled and crushed*
- *7.5 ml (1½ tsp) chilli sauce*
- *30 ml (2 tbsp) chopped fresh coriander*
- *vegetable oil for frying*
- *coarse salt, to serve*

1 Cut the pumpkin flesh into thick slices about 10 cm (5 inches) long and 1 cm (½ inch) wide. Steam for 8-10 minutes or until only just tender. Remove from the steamer and cool.

2 Place the flour, salt, baking powder, cumin seeds and ground cumin in a bowl and mix well. Make a well in the centre, add the egg yolk and gradually stir in 175 ml (6 fl oz) water to form a smooth batter, adding a little extra if necessary. Stir in the onion, garlic, chilli sauce and chopped coriander. Stiffly whisk the egg white and fold lightly into the batter.

3 One-third fill a deep-fat fryer with oil and heat to 180°C (350°F) or until hot enough to brown a cube of bread in 30 seconds. Using two forks, dip a few slices of pumpkin into the batter to coat evenly and place in the hot oil. Fry for 1-1½ minutes, turning frequently, until the fritters are crisp, golden brown and cooked through.

4 Drain on crumpled absorbent kitchen paper and keep warm while cooking the remaining pumpkin in the same way. Serve hot, sprinkled with coarse salt.

VARIATION Button mushrooms are also extremely good cooked this way.

NOTE This is an excellent way of using up the flesh scooped out of a pumpkin lantern.

SQUASH WITH NUTTY GINGERED CRUMBS

PREPARATION TIME 15 minutes
COOKING TIME 15 minutes
FREEZING Not suitable
☉

SERVES 4
- *1.4 kg (3 lb) butternut squash, peeled and cut into large chunks*
- *125 g (4 oz) butter*
- *125 g (4 oz) fresh breadcrumbs*
- *5 cm (2 inch) piece fresh root ginger, peeled and chopped*

550 CALS/SERVING
- *2 garlic cloves, peeled and crushed*
- *50 g (2 oz) pine nuts*
- *60 ml (4 tbsp) chopped fresh parsley*
- *salt and pepper*

1 Boil the squash pieces in water until just tender. Drain well and keep warm.
2 Meanwhile, heat the butter in a frying pan, add the breadcrumbs with the ginger, garlic and pine nuts and fry for about 5 minutes until golden. Add the parsley and season to taste. Stir the breadcrumb mixture into the squash and serve.

PARSNIP AND CARROT AU GRATIN

PREPARATION TIME 15 minutes
COOKING TIME 25 minutes
FREEZING Not suitable
♡

SERVES 4-6
- *450 g (1 lb) parsnips, peeled and coarsely chopped*
- *450 g (1 lb) carrots, peeled and coarsely chopped*
- *600 ml (1 pint) chicken stock*

195-130 CALS/SERVING
- *salt and pepper*
- *25 g (1 oz) butter*
- *50 g (2 oz) fresh breadcrumbs*
- *chopped fresh parsley, to garnish*

1 Put the parsnips and carrots in a saucepan with the stock and season with salt and pepper to taste. Bring to the boil, cover and simmer the vegetables gently for 15-20 minutes until they are well cooked. Drain and cool slightly.
2 Purée the vegetables in a blender or rub through a sieve. Add the butter and place in a flameproof dish. Sprinkle the breadcrumbs over the surface and cook under a hot grill until the top turns golden brown. Garnish with parsley.

CAULIFLOWER IN CURRY SAUCE

PREPARATION TIME 15 minutes
COOKING TIME About 20 minutes
FREEZING Not suitable

🕐

SERVES 4

- *1 large cauliflower*
- *90 ml (6 tbsp) ghee or vegetable oil*
- *5 ml (1 tsp) black mustard seeds*
- *5 ml (1 tsp) cumin seeds*
- *2.5 cm (1 inch) piece fresh root ginger, peeled and finely chopped*
- *1 small onion, peeled and finely chopped*
- *5 ml (1 tsp) salt*

260 CALS/SERVING

- *5 ml (1 tsp) ground turmeric*
- *3 tomatoes, skinned and finely chopped*
- *1 small green chilli, deseeded and finely chopped*
- *2.5 ml (½ tsp) sugar*
- *30 ml (2 tbsp) chopped fresh coriander*

1 Divide the cauliflower into small florets, discarding the green leaves and tough stalks. Wash well and dry on absorbent kitchen paper.
2 Heat the ghee or oil in a heavy-based saucepan or flameproof casserole. Add the mustard seeds and, when they begin to pop, stir in the cumin seeds, ginger, onion, salt and turmeric. Fry for 2-3 minutes, stirring constantly.
3 Add the cauliflower and mix well to coat with the spice mixture. Stir in the tomatoes, chopped green chilli, sugar and half of the chopped coriander. Cover the pan tightly with a lid and cook gently for 15 minutes or until the cauliflower is tender but not mushy.
4 Uncover the pan and boil rapidly for 1-2 minutes to thicken the sauce. Transfer to a warmed serving dish and sprinkle with the remaining chopped coriander. Serve immediately.

NOTE This spicy dish makes an excellent addition to an Indian meal. Alternatively serve on its own accompanied by chapatis, as a quick and tasty supper dish.

SWEDE AND ORANGE PUREE

PREPARATION TIME 15 minutes
COOKING TIME 30 minutes
FREEZING Suitable (stage 2)

♡ ❄

SERVES 4

- *1.1 kg (2½ lb) swede, peeled and sliced quite thinly*
- *salt and pepper*
- *25 g (1 oz) butter or margarine*
- *finely grated rind of 1 orange*

100 CALS/SERVING

- *30 ml (2 tbsp) orange juice*
- *45 ml (3 tbsp) soured cream*
- *parsley, to garnish*

1 Put the swede into a saucepan, cover with cold salted water and bring to the boil. Cook for about 20 minutes, until quite tender. Allow to drain thoroughly in a colander for several minutes.
2 Mash the swede, then add the butter, seasoning and grated orange rind. Stir over a moderate heat for several minutes until thoroughly hot and all excess moisture has been driven off.
3 Stir in the orange juice and the soured cream. Reheat gently, stirring all the time to prevent the purée sticking to the pan. Sprinkle with pepper and garnish with parsley.

WILD MUSHROOM AND LENTIL SALAD

PREPARATION TIME 15 minutes
COOKING TIME 5 minutes
FREEZING Not suitable
♡ ⏲

SERVES 4

80 CALS/SERVING

- *5 ml (1 tsp) walnut oil*
- *50 g (2 oz) lean smoked back bacon, cut into strips*
- *350 g (12 oz) brown-cap or wild mushrooms, halved if necessary*
- *salt and pepper*
- *5 ml (1 tsp) fresh tarragon, chopped*
- *150 ml (5 fl oz) low-fat bio natural yogurt*
- *5 ml (1 tsp) clear honey*
- *pinch of cayenne pepper*
- *selection of salad leaves, such as rocket, endive, lollo rosso*
- *50 g (2 oz) alfalfa sprouts*
- *125 g (4 oz) sprouting lentils*

1 Gently heat the walnut oil in a sauté pan and cook the bacon strips until crisp. Remove with a slotted spoon and drain on absorbent kitchen paper. Add the mushrooms to the pan, sauté until slightly softened and season to taste. Remove with a slotted spoon and drain on absorbent kitchen paper, reserving the pan juices to add to the dressing.
2 Combine the tarragon, yogurt, honey and pan juices. Season with salt and a pinch of cayenne pepper to taste.
3 Arrange the salad leaves, alfalfa sprouts, lentils, bacon and mushrooms on four plates. Spoon a little dressing on the side and serve the remainder separately.

SPICED COLESLAW WITH PECANS

PREPARATION TIME 15 minutes, plus standing
FREEZING Not suitable

SERVES 4

340 CALS/SERVING

- *350 g (12 oz) white cabbage, finely sliced*
- *2 25 g (8 oz) carrots, peeled and coarsely grated*
- *2-3 celery sticks, finely sliced*
- *50 g (2 oz) pecans or walnuts (optional)*
- *paprika, for sprinkling*
- *chervil or parsley sprigs, to garnish*

DRESSING
- *75 ml (5 tbsp) mayonnaise*
- *30 ml (2 tbsp) olive oil*
- *30 ml (2 tbsp) wine vinegar*
- *5 ml (1 tsp) chilli powder*
- *10 ml (2 tsp) mango chutney (optional)*
- *4 drops of Tabasco sauce*
- *coarse sea salt and pepper*

1 Combine the cabbage, carrots and celery in a large bowl.
2 To make the dressing, put all of the ingredients into a screw-topped jar and shake vigorously to combine.
3 Pour the dressing over the salad and toss well. Cover and leave to stand for several hours or overnight if possible, in a cool place.
4 Just before serving, toss the pecans into the salad. Sprinkle with a little paprika and garnish with chervil or parsley.

NOTE If possible make this salad the day before, or at least several hours ahead, to enable the flavours of the dressing to be absorbed.

VARIATION To make the dressing suitable for vegans, substitute 125 g (4 oz) tofu for the mayonnaise. Put all of the dressing ingredients into a blender or food processor and work until smooth, adding a little more oil to thin if necessary.

VEGETABLE AND APPLE STIR-FRY

PREPARATION TIME 15 minutes
COOKING TIME 15 minutes
FREEZING Not suitable

⊙

SERVES 4
- *60 ml (4 tbsp) vegetable oil*
- *1 garlic clove, peeled and crushed*
- *350 g (12 oz) small leeks, trimmed and sliced*
- *4 sticks green celery, sliced*
- *225 g (8 oz) courgettes, sliced*
- *1 red pepper, deseeded and chopped*

285 CALS/SERVING
- *30 ml (2 tbsp) medium curry paste*
- *5 ml (1 tsp) ground ginger*
- *15 ml (1 tbsp) clear honey*
- *2 crisp, green eating apples*
- *50 g (2 oz) unsalted cashew nuts*
- *salt and pepper*
- *juice of 1 lemon*
- *flat-leaf parsley, to garnish*

1 Heat the oil in a non-stick sauté pan and cook the garlic for a few seconds. Stir in the vegetables and cook over a high heat for 10 minutes, stirring occasionally.

2 Add the curry paste, ginger, honey and 45 ml (3 tbsp) water and stir until smooth.

3 Roughly chop the apples. Add to the pan with the cashew nuts and plenty of seasoning. Cook for a further 5 minutes or until the vegetables are just tender but retain some bite. Squeeze lemon juice over to serve. Garnish with flat-leaf parsley.

TIP
When stir-frying, always make sure that the oil is sizzling before you add the ingredients. Keep the food on the move to ensure even cooking.

APPLE AND FIG STRUDEL

PREPARATION TIME 25 minutes
COOKING TIME 30 minutes
FREEZING Suitable
♡ ✻

SERVES 6

- *125 g (4 oz) no-soak dried figs, roughly chopped*
- *grated rind and juice of 1 lemon*
- *25 g (1 oz) fresh white breadcrumbs*
- *450 g (1 lb) cooking apples*

160 CALS/SERVING

- *4 sheets filo pastry, about 125 g (4 oz) total weight*
- *25 g (1 oz) low-fat spread*
- *5 ml (1 tsp) caster sugar*
- *icing sugar, to dust*

1 Place the figs in a large bowl with the lemon rind and juice and the breadcrumbs.
2 Peel, quarter, core and thinly slice the apples. Mix the apples with the figs.
3 Lay two pieces of filo pastry side by side on a clean tea towel, overlapping the longest edges by about 5 cm (2 inches). Brush with a little melted low-fat spread. Top with the other two sheets of pastry and brush again.
4 Place the apple mixture along the longest edge and roll up, using the tea towel to help you. Roll onto a non-stick baking sheet, curling it slightly to fit the sheet. Brush with the remaining fat and sprinkle the sugar over.
5 Bake at 190°C (375°F) mark 5 for 30-35 minutes or until the pastry is golden brown and the apple is quite soft. Cover with foil if necessary. Serve hot, dusted lightly with icing sugar.

NOTE Using low-fat spread reduces the calorie content slightly, helping to make this delicious strudel a surprisingly healthy dessert.

VARIATION *Apple, Apricot and Almond Strudel*
Replace the figs with 125 g (4 oz) no-soak dried apricots. Add 30 ml (2 tbsp) ground almonds and 2.5 ml (½ tsp) ground cinnamon to the filling. Sprinkle 15 g (½ oz) flaked almonds over before baking.

BRAMLEY APPLES WITH GINGER

PREPARATION TIME 15 minutes, plus soaking
COOKING TIME 50 minutes
FREEZING Not suitable

SERVES 4

- *175 g (6 oz) no-soak dried prunes*
- *150 ml (5 fl oz) apple juice*
- *15 g (½ oz) stem ginger, finely chopped and 15 ml (1 tbsp) syrup from the stem ginger jar*

275 CALS/SERVING

- *grated rind and juice of 1 lemon*
- *about 150 g (5 oz) soft light brown sugar*
- *4 small Bramley apples, about 225 g (8 oz) each*

1 Snip the prunes into the apple juice and leave to soak for 30 minutes.
2 Mix the stem ginger with the ginger syrup, lemon rind and juice and 125 g (4 oz) sugar. Strain the prunes, reserving the juice, and add the prunes to the ginger mixture.
3 Wash and core the apples. Cut the skin at the centre of the apple to stop the fruit bursting in the oven. Place in an ovenproof dish.
4 Fill the centre of each apple with the prune mixture, sprinkling any extra over the top. Pour the reserved apple juice over and sprinkle with a little sugar. Cover loosely.
5 Bake at 200°C (400°F) mark 6 for about 50 minutes. Serve with the juices spooned over.

> *TIP*
> If you don't have stem ginger in your store-cupboard, use 2.5 ml (½ tsp) ground ginger and omit the ginger syrup.

ALMOND TARTE TATIN

PREPARATION TIME 15 minutes, plus chilling
COOKING TIME 35 minutes
FREEZING Not suitable

SERVES 6

380 CALS/SERVING

- *125 g (4 oz) white plain flour*
- *pinch of salt*
- *25 g (1 oz) ground almonds*
- *50 g (2 oz) caster sugar*
- *125 g (4 oz) butter*
- *2 egg yolks*
- *few drops almond essence*

- *125 g (4 oz) soft light brown sugar*
- *5 Cox's Orange Pippins, about 700 g (1½ lb) total weight*
- *50 g (2 oz) toasted flaked almonds*

1 Put the flour, salt, ground almonds, caster sugar and 50 g (2 oz) of the butter in a food processor and process until the mixture resembles fine breadcrumbs. Add the egg yolks and almond essence and process until the mixture just comes together. Knead to a smooth dough on a floured surface. Wrap and chill for about 1 hour.
2 Peel, quarter and core the apples. Melt the remaining butter in a non-stick frying pan, add the brown sugar and slowly dissolve. Increase the heat slightly and stir for about 1 minute or until the mixture becomes smooth and thick.
3 Add the apples and flaked almonds and cook over a medium heat, stirring occasionally, for 10 minutes or until the apples soften slightly and the sugar mixture caramelizes. Pour into a 2.5 cm (1 inch) deep, 20 cm (8 inch) round non-stick sandwich tin. Leave to cool.
4 Roll out the chilled dough to a round slightly larger than the sandwich tin. Place on top of the apples, tucking the edges down the sides of the tin.
5 Bake at 190°C (375°F) mark 5 for about 20 minutes or until the pastry is golden brown. Leave to cool for 10 minutes. Invert on to a serving plate and serve.

NOTE The cake tin must be non-stick or the metal may taint the apples.

APPLE AND BLACKBERRY UPSIDE-DOWN PUDDING

PREPARATION TIME 20 minutes
COOKING TIME 1 hour
FREEZING Suitable
✳

SERVES 8

TOPPING
- *90 ml (6 tbsp) raspberry jam*
- *350 g (12 oz) blackberries or loganberries*
- *1 large eating apple, peeled, cored and chopped*

CAKE
- *75 g (3 oz) white self-raising flour*
- *75 g (3 oz) wholemeal self-*

225 CALS/SERVING
- *5 ml (1 tsp) baking powder*
- *large pinch of salt*
- *1 egg*
- *finely grated rind and juice of 1 large orange*
- *30 ml (2 tbsp) milk*
- *75 g (3 oz) butter or margarine*
- *75 g (3 oz) caster sugar*

1 To make the topping, gently heat the jam in a small saucepan and pour into a greased 23 cm (9 inch) round spring-release cake tin. Wash the blackberries and arrange with the apple evenly over the base of the cake tin.

2 To make the cake, put all the ingredients into a large bowl and beat until smooth and glossy. Carefully spread over the fruit

3 Bake in the oven at 190ºC (375ºF) mark 5 for about 1 hour until the pudding is well risen and firm to the touch. Cover the top with a double

sheet of greaseproof paper after 40 minutes to prevent overbrowning.

4 Leave the pudding to cool in the tin for 5 minutes, then turn out and serve.

PLUM CUSTARD BAKE

PREPARATION TIME 10 minutes
COOKING TIME 40 minutes
FREEZING Not suitable
♡

SERVES 6
- *450 g (1 lb) plums*
- *75 g (3 oz) caster sugar*
- *3 eggs*
- *300 ml (10 fl oz) milk*
- *grated zest of ½ lemon*

175 CALS/SERVING
- *5 ml (1 tsp) ground ginger*
- *5 ml (1 tsp) vanilla essence*
- *45 ml (3 tbsp) clear honey*

1 Halve and stone the plums, then arrange, cut-side down, in a round, shallow 1.1 litre (2 pint) ovenproof dish. Sprinkle with 30 ml (2 tbsp) of the sugar.

2 Whisk the eggs with all the remaining ingredients except the honey to make a smooth custard. Pour over the fruit.

3 Place the dish in a roasting tin filled with enough hot water to reach halfway up the side of the dish. Cook at 150°C (300°F) mark 2 for 40 minutes or until just set. Serve immediately, drizzled with warmed clear honey.

VARIATION Use greengages instead of plums and replace the ginger with grated nutmeg to taste.

POACHED PEARS WITH APRICOTS

PREPARATION TIME 8 minutes
COOKING TIME 5-10 minutes
FREEZING Not suitable

♡ ⏲

SERVES 4

- 25 g (1 oz) butter or margarine
- 25 g (1 oz) soft brown sugar
- 15 ml (1 tbsp) lemon juice
- 700 g (1½ lb) ripe but firm pears
- 50 g (2 oz) no-soak dried apricots

195 CALS/SERVING

- 15 ml (1 tbsp) Grand Marnier or brandy
- chopped nuts, to decorate
- ice cream, to serve

1 Put the butter, sugar and lemon juice in a saucepan with 150 ml (5 fl oz) water and warm together.
2 Peel, quarter and core the pears. Halve each quarter again if large. Snip the apricots into shreds.
3 Add the pears and apricots to the syrup, cover and simmer for 5-10 minutes or until the pears are just tender. Stir in the Grand Marnier.
4 Serve hot, sprinkled with chopped nuts and topped with ice cream.

CRISPY PEAR CLAFOUTIS

PREPARATION TIME 15 minutes, plus standing
COOKING TIME 50 minutes
FREEZING Not suitable

SERVES 6

- 3 eggs
- 50 g (2 oz) white self-raising flour
- 150 g (5 oz) white plain flour
- large pinch of salt
- 5 ml (1 tsp) ground cinnamon
- 200 ml (7 fl oz) milk

270 CALS/SERVING

- 30 ml (2 tbsp) Armagnac
- 50 g (2 oz) butter
- 350 g (12 oz) ripe dessert pears
- caster and icing sugar, to serve

1 Whisk the eggs, flours, salt and cinnamon with 150 ml (5 fl oz) milk until smooth. Whisk in the remaining milk with the Armagnac. Cover and leave to stand for 2 hours.
2 Using half the butter, grease a 23 cm (9 inch) spring-release cake tin. Stand the tin on a baking sheet. Thinly slice the pears. Whisk the batter again and pour into the prepared tin. Lay the pear slices on top. Dot with the remaining butter.
3 Bake at 240°C (475°F) mark 9 for 15-20 minutes or until well risen, then lower the temperature to 220°C (425°F) mark 7 for a further 35 minutes or until risen and well browned. Dust with a mixture of caster and icing sugar to serve.

SAFFRON MERINGUES WITH BLUEBERRY SAUCE

PREPARATION TIME 25 minutes
COOKING TIME 2 hours
FREEZING Suitable
❄

SERVES 6	260 CALS/SERVING
MERINGUES	*BLUEBERRY SAUCE*

MERINGUES
- small pinch of saffron strands (optional)
- 2 egg whites
- 125 g (4 oz) caster sugar
- 200 ml (7 fl oz) crème fraîche

BLUEBERRY SAUCE
- 450 g (1 lb) blueberries
- 40 g (1½ oz) caster sugar
- 30 ml (2 tbsp) chopped fresh mint

1 Line two baking sheets with non-stick baking parchment. Put the saffron (if using) in a small bowl and pour on 15 ml (1 tbsp) boiling water. Whisk the egg whites in a large bowl until holding soft peaks. Whisk in 30 ml (2 tbsp) of the sugar, then strain in the saffron liquid and whisk again until the meringue is stiff. Fold in the remaining sugar.
2 Using two large spoons, shape the meringue mixture into 12 oval mounds on the prepared

baking sheets. Bake in the oven at 110°C (225°F) mark ¼ for about 2 hours until the meringues are well dried out. Carefully peel the meringues off the paper and leave to cool on a wire rack.
3 To make the sauce, place the blueberries in a saucepan with the sugar and 45 ml (3 tbsp) water and cook over a low heat for 5-7 minutes until they are just tender, but still holding their shape. Using a slotted spoon, remove about one quarter of the blueberries and press through a fine sieve into a large bowl. Stir in the rest of the blueberries with the chopped mint and leave to cool, stirring occasionally.
4 About 1 hour before serving, sandwich the meringues together with the crème fraîche. Pile on to one or two serving dishes, cover and chill until ready to serve. Pour the sauce into a jug and serve with the meringues.

VARIATION *Cinnamon Meringues with Red Sauce* Omit the saffron, and add 5 ml (1 tsp) ground cinnamon to the egg whites with the sugar. Replace the blueberries with 450 g (1 lb) cherries, raspberries or strawberries.

CHOCOLATE TRUFFLE CAKE

PREPARATION TIME 25 minutes, plus setting
COOKING TIME 20 minutes
FREEZING Suitable
❄

SERVES 16	580 CALS/SERVING

- 150 g (5 oz) sugar
- 90 g (3½ oz) blanched whole almonds, toasted
- 23 cm (9 inch) round chocolate sponge
- 90 ml (6 tbsp) Tia Maria

- 600 g (1 lb 6 oz) plain chocolate
- 600 ml (1 pint) double cream
- 3 egg yolks
- 40 g (1½ oz) caster sugar

1 Melt the sugar in a heavy-based saucepan over a gentle heat. Add the almonds and cook until dark golden. Carefully pour onto an oiled baking sheet – the pan and caramel will be very hot. Set aside to cool.
2 Line the sides of a 23 cm (9 inch) spring-release cake tin with non-stick baking parchment. Carefully slice a thin circle of chocolate sponge, about 5 mm (¼ inch) deep. Place cut side up in

the base of the tin. Push down firmly and use pieces of sponge to patch up any holes (any remaining sponge can be frozen). Drizzle 30 ml (2 tbsp) Tia Maria over and set aside.

3 Break the chocolate into a heatproof bowl and add 150 ml (5 fl oz) cream. Melt the chocolate over a pan of gently simmering water. Do not stir.

4 Meanwhile, using an electric whisk, whisk together the egg yolks and caster sugar in a bowl for 10 minutes or until pale, thick and creamy.

5 Break the almond caramel into small pieces. Process in a blender or food processor until it resembles coarse breadcrumbs.

6 With a metal spoon, fold the melted chocolate into the egg mixture and mix well. Fold in the almond caramel and the remaining Tia Maria.

7 Lightly whip the remaining double cream until it just holds its shape, then fold it into the chocolate mixture. Pour into the cake tin. Set in the refrigerator overnight.

8 To serve, remove from the tin, discarding the lining paper, and cut with a sharp, hot knife.

NOTE For an autumnal decoration, melt 50 g (2 oz) dark, milk and white chocolate in separate bowls. Coat about 10 opened cape gooseberries in chocolate. Heat 50 g (2 oz) sugar and melt until golden brown. Coat about 5 cape gooseberries in the caramel. Decorate the cake with coated and fresh cape gooseberries. Fix greaseproof paper around the base, then tie raffia over it.

HONEY-TOASTED RICE

PREPARATION TIME 10 minutes
COOKING TIME 3 hours
FREEZING Not suitable

SERVES 4
- *600 ml (1 pint) milk*
- *300 ml (10 fl oz) single cream*
- *75 g (3 oz) pudding rice*
- *knob of butter*
- *30 ml (2 tbsp) caster sugar*
- *1.25 ml (¼ tsp)*

435 CALS/SERVING
- *large pinch of grated nutmeg*
- *50 g (2 oz) flaked or shredded almonds, roughly chopped or cut into thin shreds*
- *45 ml (3 tbsp) clear honey*
- *15 ml (1 tbsp)*

1 Mix together the first seven ingredients. Pour into a 5 cm (2 inch) deep 1.4 litre (2½ pint) ovenproof dish. Place in a roasting tin with enough warm water to come halfway up the side of the dish.

2 Cook at 150°C (300°F) mark 2 for about 2½-3 hours or until lightly set and golden. Turn off the oven and leave the pudding inside for about 20 minutes.

3 Scatter the almonds over the pudding. Mix together the honey and lemon juice and drizzle over the nuts. Place under a hot grill until a golden brown colour. Serve hot or cold.

TIP
Keep a whole nutmeg for grating in your store-cupboard, rather than a tub of ready-grated nutmeg. The flavour is fresh and cleaner and a single nutmeg will last for years.

CINNAMON COFFEE CAKE

PREPARATION TIME 20 minutes
COOKING TIME 35-40 minutes
FREEZING Suitable

✳

MAKES 8 SLICES
- *125 g (4 oz) butter*
- *200 g (7 oz) granulated sugar*
- *2 eggs*
- *150 ml (5 fl oz) soured cream*
- *10 ml (2 tsp) vanilla essence*
- *125 g (4 oz) white plain flour*

420 CALS/SLICE
- *10 ml (2 tsp) baking powder*
- *pinch of salt*
- *150 g (5 oz) walnuts or pecan nuts, chopped*
- *10 ml (2 tsp) ground cinnamon*

1 Grease and base-line a deep 20 cm (8 inch) round cake tin. Lightly dust with flour.
2 Cream together the butter with 175 g (6 oz) sugar. Beat in the eggs, soured cream and vanilla essence. Fold in the flour, the baking powder and salt. Do not overbeat. Mix together the remaining sugar, nuts and cinnamon.
3 Spoon half the cake mixture into the prepared tin. Sprinkle over half the nut mixture. Add the remaining cake mixture and top with the rest of the nuts and sugar.
4 Bake at 180°C (350°F) mark 4 for about 35-40 minutes. Serve warm or cold.

CRUMBLY APPLE AND CHEESE CAKE

PREPARATION TIME 20 minutes
COOKING TIME 50 minutes-1 hour
FREEZING Suitable

✳

MAKES 10 SLICES
- *175 g (6 oz) white self-raising flour*
- *5 ml (1 tsp) baking powder*
- *75 g (3 oz) light muscovado sugar*
- *50 g (2 oz) raisins*
- *50 g (2 oz) sultanas*
- *50 g (2 oz) brazil nuts, chopped*

A345 CALS/SLICE
- *575 g (1¼ lb) dessert apples, peeled, cored and thinly sliced*
- *2 eggs*
- *90 ml (3 fl oz) sunflower oil*
- *225 g (8 oz) Caerphilly cheese*
- *icing sugar*

1 Grease a 5 cm (2 inch) deep, 23 cm (9 inch) round loose-based flan tin.
2 Sift the flour and baking powder into a bowl. Stir in the sugar, raisins, sultanas, nuts and apples. Beat the eggs with the oil and add to the dry ingredients. Mix well together.
3 Turn half the mixture into the prepared tin and level the surface. Crumble the cheese over, then cover with the remaining cake mixture. Roughly spread the mixture to the edges of the tin.
4 Bake at 180°C (350°F) mark 4 for 50 minutes to 1 hour until golden and just firm. Leave to cool in the tin for 10 minutes, then transfer to a wire rack. Serve warm, sprinkled with icing sugar.

ALMOND, CHOCOLATE AND SWEET POTATO LOAF

PREPARATION TIME 20 minutes
COOKING TIME 1-1¼ hours
FREEZING Suitable
❄

MAKES 8-10 SLICES   435-350 CALS/SLICE

- *225 g (8 oz) sweet potatoes, peeled and cut into chunks*
- *125 g (4 oz) soft margarine*
- *125 g (4 oz) light muscovado sugar*
- *5 ml (1 tsp) vanilla essence*
- *2 eggs*
- *160 g (5½ oz) white self-raising flour*
- *15 g (½ oz) cocoa powder*
- *5 ml (1 tsp) ground mixed spice*
- *2.5 ml (½ tsp) bicarbonate of soda*
- *30 ml (2 tbsp) milk*
- *125 g (4 oz) milk chocolate, roughly chopped*
- *75 g (3 oz) flaked almonds, lightly toasted*
- *icing sugar, for dusting*

1 Add the sweet potatoes to a pan of cold water, bring to the boil and cook for 15 minutes or until softened. Drain well, then mash with a potato masher.
2 Grease a 900 g (2 lb) loaf tin and line the base and long sides with a strip of greaseproof paper.
3 Put the margarine, sugar, vanilla essence and eggs in a bowl. Sift the flour, cocoa, mixed spice and bicarbonate of soda into the bowl. Add the milk and beat well until smooth and creamy.
4 Stir in the mashed sweet potato, chopped chocolate and 50 g (2 oz) of the toasted almonds. Turn the mixture into the prepared tin and level the surface. Sprinkle with the remaining almonds.
5 Bake at 170°C (325°F) mark 3 for about 1-1¼ hours until well risen and just firm to the touch. Leave in the tin for 10 minutes, then transfer to a wire rack to cool. Serve dusted with icing sugar.

NOTE Cook this cake as soon as you have mixed it, as the bicarbonate of soda is activated on blending.

VARIATION *Chocolate, Orange and Parsnip Loaf*
Replace the sweet potatoes with parsnips. Substitute 2.5 ml (½ tsp) ground coriander for the mixed spice, and add the finely grated rind of 1 orange.

GINGER CAKE

PREPARATION TIME 15 minutes
COOKING TIME 1 hour
FREEZING Suitable
♡ ❄

MAKES ABOUT 25 SLICES   140 CALS/SLICE

- *225 g (8 oz) white plain flour*
- *pinch of salt*
- *2.5 ml (½ tsp) bicarbonate of soda*
- *15 ml (1 tbsp) ground ginger*
- *5 ml (1 tsp) ground allspice*
- *25 g (1 oz) medium oatmeal*
- *125 g (4 oz) black treacle*
- *150 g (5 oz) golden syrup*
- *175 g (6 oz) butter*
- *50 g (2 oz) soft dark brown sugar*
- *150 ml (5 fl oz) milk*
- *2 eggs, beaten*
- *125 g (4 oz) stem ginger, drained and finely chopped*

1 Grease and line the base of a 5 cm (2 inch) deep, 20 cm (8 inch) square cake tin.
2 Sift the flour, salt, bicarbonate of soda, ground ginger and allspice into a bowl. Add the oatmeal.
3 Put the treacle, syrup, butter, sugar and milk in a saucepan and heat gently, stirring until melted.
4 Make a well in the centre of the dry ingredients. Add the eggs and stem ginger with the treacle mixture. Beat until smooth. Pour into the prepared tin.
5 Bake at 180°C (350°F) mark 4 for about 1 hour. Cool in the tin for 5 minutes, then cool on a wire rack. Store for up to one week.

APPLE AND MINT JELLY

PREPARATION TIME 30 minutes, plus standing
COOKING TIME About 1¼ hours
FREEZING Not suitable

- *2.3 kg (5 lb) cooking apples, such as Bramleys*
- *few large mint sprigs*
- *1.1 litres (2 pints) distilled white vinegar*
- *sugar (see method)*

35-40 CALS/15 ML (1 TBSP)
- *90-120 ml (6-8 tbsp) chopped mint*
- *few drops of green food colouring (optional)*

1 Remove any bruised parts from the apples, then roughly chop into chunks without peeling or coring. Put the apples in a preserving pan with 1.1 litres (2 pints) water and the mint sprigs.
2 Bring to the boil, then simmer gently for about 45 minutes or until soft and pulpy, stirring from time to time to prevent sticking. Add the vinegar and boil for a further 5 minutes.
3 Spoon the apple pulp into a jelly bag suspended over a large bowl and leave to drip through for at least 12 hours.
4 Discard any pulp remaining in the jelly bag. Measure the extract and return to the preserving pan with 450 g (1 lb) sugar for each 600 ml (1 pint) extract.
5 Heat gently, stirring, until the sugar has dissolved, then boil rapidly for about 10 minutes or until setting point is reached. Remove any scum with a slotted spoon.
6 Stir in the chopped mint and colouring, if using. Cool slightly, stir well to distribute the mint, then pot and cover in the usual way (see page 77).

NOTE It is not practicable to state the exact yield in jelly recipes because the ripeness of the fruit and the time allowed for dripping both affect the quantity of juice obtained. As a rough guide, for each 450 g (1 lb) sugar added, a yield of about 700 g (1½ lb) will result.

MARROW AND APRICOT JAM

PREPARATION TIME 10 minutes, plus soaking
COOKING TIME About 1 hour
FREEZING Not suitable

MAKES ABOUT
2.3 KG (5 LB)
- *900 g (2 lb) marrow, peeled, deseeded and cut into squares (prepared weight)*
- *225 g (8 oz) dried apricots, soaked overnight and drained*

40 CALS/15 ML (1 TBSP)
- *grated rind and juice of 2 lemons*
- *1.4 kg (3 lb) sugar*

1 Steam the marrow for about 15 minutes or until tender, then mash.
2 Put the apricots in a preserving pan with 900 ml (1½ pints) water and cook for about 30 minutes or until soft.
3 Add the marrow pulp to the apricots with the lemon rind, lemon juice and sugar. Heat gently until the sugar has dissolved, stirring to prevent sticking. Bring to the boil and boil rapidly for 15-20 minutes or until setting point is reached.
4 Remove any scum with a slotted spoon, then pot and cover in the usual way (see page 77).

NOTE For guidance on testing for setting point, see page 77.

SWEETCORN RELISH

PREPARATION TIME 15 minutes
COOKING TIME About 35 minutes
FREEZING Not suitable

MAKES ABOUT
2.3 KG (5 LB)

15 CALS/15 ML (1 TBSP)

- 6 corn cobs, trimmed, leaves and silk removed
- ½ a small white cabbage, roughly chopped
- 2 onions, peeled and halved
- 1½ red peppers, deseeded and quartered

- 10 ml (2 tsp) salt
- 30 ml (2 tbsp) white plain flour
- 2.5 ml (½ tsp) ground turmeric
- 175 g (6 oz) sugar
- 10 ml (2 tsp) mustard powder
- 600 ml (1 pint) distilled vinegar

1 Cook the corn cobs in boiling salted water for 3 minutes, then drain. Using a sharp knife, cut the corn from the cobs. Coarsely mince the cabbage, onions and red peppers and combine with the corn.
2 Blend the salt, flour, turmeric, sugar and mustard together in a saucepan, then gradually stir in the vinegar. Heat gently, stirring, until the sugar has dissolved, then bring to the boil. Reduce the heat, add the vegetables and simmer for 25-30 minutes, stirring occasionally.
3 Pot and cover in the usual way (see page 77).

DAMSON CHUTNEY

PREPARATION TIME 30 minutes
COOKING TIME 1½-2 hours
FREEZING Not suitable

MAKES ABOUT
1.8 KG (4 LB)

35 CALS/15 ML (1 TBSP)

- 1.6 kg (3½ lb) damsons, washed
- 2 onions, peeled and chopped
- 1 garlic clove, peeled and crushed
- 225 g (8 oz) seedless raisins, chopped
- 125 g (4 oz) stoned dates, chopped

- 700 g (1½ lb) dark soft brown sugar
- 1.4 litres (2½ pints) malt vinegar
- 15 g (½ oz) salt
- 25 g (1 oz) ground ginger
- 1.25 ml (¼ tsp) ground allspice

1 Mix all the ingredients together in a large saucepan. Heat gently, stirring, until the sugar has dissolved, then bring to the boil. Reduce the heat and simmer, uncovered, for 1½-2 hours, stirring occasionally, until no excess liquid remains and the mixture is thick. Scoop out the damson stones with a slotted spoon.
2 Pot and cover in the usual way (see page 77).

VARIATION If preferred, plums can be used instead of damsons.

BASIC RECIPES

Making your own stocks and pastry will give recipes that extra depth of flavour, while homemade mayonnaise and bread will give everyday meals a culinary lift.

VEGETABLE STOCK

PREPARATION TIME 15 minutes
COOKING TIME 1¾ hours
FREEZING Suitable

MAKES 1.1 LITRES (2 PINTS)
- *30 ml (2 tbsp) vegetable oil*
- *1 onion, peeled and finely chopped*
- *1 carrot, peeled and diced*
- *50 g (2 oz) turnip, peeled and diced*
- *50 g (2 oz) parsnip, peeled and diced*
- *4 celery sticks, chopped*
- *vegetable trimmings, such as celery tops, cabbage leaves, mushroom peelings, tomato skins*
- *1 bouquet garni*
- *6 black peppercorns*
- *a little salt*

1 Heat the oil in a saucepan, add the onion and fry gently for about 5 minutes until lightly coloured.
2 Add the other vegetables to the pan with the trimmings and 1.7 litres (3 pints) water. Add the bouquet garni and peppercorns. Season with salt.
3 Bring to the boil, partially cover and simmer for 1½ hours, skimming occasionally.
4 Strain the stock and leave to cool. Cover and store in the refrigerator. Use within 1-2 days.

BEEF STOCK

PREPARATION TIME 15 minutes,
COOKING TIME 4½-5½ hours
FREEZING Suitable

MAKES 900 ML (1½ PINTS)
- *450 g (1 lb) shin of beef, cut into pieces*
- *450 g (1 lb) marrow bones or knuckle of veal, chopped*
- *1 bouquet garni*
- *1 onion, peeled and sliced*
- *1 carrot, peeled and sliced*
- *1 celery stick, sliced*
- *2.5 ml (½ tsp) salt*

1 To give a good flavour and colour, brown the meat and bones in the oven before using them. Place in a roasting tin and cook at 220°C (425°F)

mark 7 for 30-40 minutes until well browned.
2 Put the bones and meat in a saucepan with 1.7 litres (3 pints) water, the bouquet garni, vegetables and salt. Bring to the boil and remove any scum.
3 Partially cover and simmer for 4-5 hours.
4 Strain and, when cold, remove all traces of fat.

CHICKEN STOCK

PREPARATION TIME 15 minutes
COOKING TIME 2-3 hours
FREEZING Suitable

MAKES 1.1 LITRES (2 PINTS)
- *1 chicken carcass, bones and trimmings from a roast chicken*
- *1 onion, peeled and sliced*
- *1 carrot, peeled and sliced*
- *1 celery stick, sliced*
- *1 bouquet garni*
- *1 bay leaf*
- *salt*

1 Break up the chicken carcass and put in a large saucepan with any skin and meat attached, plus other bones and trimmings.
2 Add 1.7 litres (3 pints) water, the onion, carrot, celery, bouquet garni, bay leaf and a little salt. Bring to the boil, then skim.
3 Partially cover and simmer for 2-3 hours.
4 Strain and, when cold, remove all traces of fat.

FISH STOCK

PREPARATION TIME 10 minutes
COOKING TIME 20 minutes
FREEZING Suitable

MAKES 900 ML (1½ PINTS)
- *450-750 g (1-1½ lb) fish bones and trimmings*
- *salt*
- *1 bouquet garni*
- *1 onion, peeled and sliced*

1 Put the fish bones and trimmings into a saucepan, cover with 900 ml (1½ pints) water and add a little salt. Bring to the boil, then skim.
2 Reduce the heat and add the bouquet garni and

onion. Cover and simmer for 20 minutes.
3 Strain and leave to cool. Use on the same day, or store in the refrigerator for not more than 2 days.

SHORTCRUST PASTRY

PREPARATION TIME 10 minutes, plus resting
FREEZING Suitable

For shortcrust pastry, the proportion of flour to fat is 2:1, or twice the quantity. Therefore, for a recipe using quantities of shortcrust pastry other than 225 g (8 oz), simply use half the quantity of fat to the flour weight specified.

MAKES 225 G (8 OZ) — **175 CALS/25 G (1 OZ)**
- *225 g (8 oz) white plain flour*
- *pinch of salt*
- *125 g (4 oz) butter or margarine, chilled and diced*

1 Mix flour and salt together in a bowl. Add the fat to the flour. Using your fingertips, rub the fat lightly into the flour until the mixture resembles fine breadcrumbs.
2 Add 45-60 ml (3-4 tbsp) chilled water, sprinkling it evenly over the surface.
3 Stir in with a round-bladed knife until the mixture begins to stick together in large lumps. Collect the dough mixture together to form a ball.
4 Knead lightly for a few seconds to give a firm, smooth dough; do not overhandle the dough. Wrap in clingfilm or greaseproof paper and rest in the refrigerator for about 30 minutes.
5 To roll out the pastry, sprinkle a very little flour on a work surface and the rolling pin (not on the pastry) and roll out the dough evenly in one direction only, turning it occasionally. The usual thickness is 3 mm (1/8 inch). Do not pull or stretch the pastry.

VARIATION *Walnut Shortcrust Pastry* Follow the recipe for Shortcrust Pastry, stirring in 40 g (1½ oz) very finely chopped, shelled walnuts before adding the water.

BAKING BLIND

If a recipe for a flan or tart instructs you to bake blind, it means that you should partially or completely bake the pastry case before filling. To bake blind, first prick the pastry base with a fork, then line with a large piece of greaseproof paper or foil. Fill with ceramic baking beans or dried pulses. Small cases don't need lining – just prick with a fork.

For partially baked cases, bake at 200°C (400°F) mark 6 for 10-15 minutes until the case looks 'set'. Carefully remove the paper or foil and the beans and bake for a further 5 minutes until the base is firm to the touch and lightly coloured.

For completely baked cases, return to the oven for about 15 minutes until firm and golden brown.

PUFF PASTRY

PREPARATION TIME 40 minutes, plus resting
FREEZING Suitable

The richest of all the pastries, puff requires patience, practice and very light handling. Whenever possible it should be made the day before use. It is not practical to make in a quantity with less than 450 g (1 lb) flour weight. This quantity is equivalent to two 375 g (13 oz) packets.

MAKES 450 G (1 LB) — **270 CALS/25 G (1 OZ)**
- *450 g (1 lb) strong plain flour*
- *pinch of salt*
- *450 g (1 lb) butter or margarine, chilled*
- *15 ml (1 tbsp) lemon juice*

1 Mix the flour and salt together. Cut off 50 g (2 oz) of the butter and flatten the remaining butter with a rolling pin to a slab 2 cm (¾ inch) thick.
2 Cut the 50 g (2 oz) butter into small pieces, add to the flour and rub in. Using a round-bladed knife, stir in the lemon juice and about 300 ml (10 fl oz) chilled water to make a soft, elastic dough.
3 Quickly knead the dough until smooth and shape into a round. Cut through half the depth in the shape of a cross. Open out to form a star.
4 Roll out, keeping the centre four times as thick as the flaps. Place the slab of butter in the centre.
5 Fold the flaps envelope-style and press gently with a rolling pin. Roll out to a rectangle measuring about 40 x 20 cm (16 x 8 inches).
6 Fold bottom third up and top third down, keeping the edges straight. Seal edges. Wrap in greaseproof paper and rest in the refrigerator for 30 minutes.
7 Put the pastry on a lightly floured work surface with the folded edges to the sides, then repeat the rolling, folding and resting sequence 5 times.

PATE SUCREE

PREPARATION TIME 10 minutes, plus resting
FREEZING Suitable

Pâte Sucrée is the classic French rich short pastry used for sweet flans.

MAKES 125 G (4 OZ)
- *125 g (4 oz) white plain flour*
- *pinch of salt*
- *50 g (2 oz) butter (at room temperature)*

255 CALS/25 G (1 OZ)
- *2 egg yolks*
- *50 g (2 oz) caster sugar*

1 Sift the flour and salt onto a work surface. Make a well in the centre and add the butter, egg yolks and sugar.
2 Using the fingertips of one hand, pinch and work the sugar, butter and egg yolks together until well blended.
3 Gradually work in all the flour to bind the mixture together. Knead lightly until smooth, then wrap the pastry in clingfilm and leave to rest in a cool place for at least 30 minutes. Roll out as for Shortcrust Pastry (see page 75).

SWEET FLAN PASTRY

PREPARATION TIME 10 minutes, plus resting
FREEZING Suitable

This is made by the same method as shortcrust pastry, but beaten egg is used instead of water.

MAKES 125 G (4 OZ)
- *125 g (4 oz) white plain flour*
- *pinch of salt*
- *75g (3 oz) butter or margarine, chilled and diced*

250 CALS/25 G (1 OZ)
- *5 ml (1 tsp) caster sugar*
- *1 egg, beaten*

1 Sift the flour and salt into a bowl. Rub in the fat until the mixture resembles fine breadcrumbs. Stir in the sugar.
2 Add the egg, stirring with a round-bladed knife until the ingredients begin to stick together.
3 With one hand, form into a firm, smooth dough. Wrap the pastry in clingfilm and rest in a cool place for at least 30 minutes. Roll out as for Shortcrust Pastry (see page 75).

WHOLEMEAL BREAD

PREPARATION TIME 30 minutes, plus rising
COOKING TIME 35 minutes
FREEZING Suitable

MAKES 1 LOAF
- *15 g (¹/₂ oz) fresh yeast or 7 g sachet (1¹/₂ tsp) fast-action dried yeast*
- *150 ml (5 fl oz) tepid milk*
- *450 g (1 lb) wholemeal plain flour*

1700 CALS/LOAF
- *5 ml (1 tsp) salt*
- *5 ml (1 tsp) caster sugar*
- *25 g (1 oz) butter or margarine*
- *beaten egg, water or milk for glazing*

1 If using fresh yeast, blend with the milk. Mix the flour, salt and sugar in a bowl, and stir in the fast-action dried yeast if using. Rub in the butter. Make a well in centre and pour in the yeast liquid or milk and about 175 ml (6 fl oz) tepid water. Mix to a soft dough.
2 Turn out the dough onto a lightly floured surface and knead for about 10 minutes until smooth and elastic. If using fresh yeast, place in an oiled bowl and cover with oiled clingfilm. Leave to rise until doubled in size and sponge-like.
3 Knock the risen dough down, then knead again on a lightly floured surface for 3-4 minutes until smooth. Flatten the dough to an oblong the length of a 900 g (2 lb) loaf tin but three times as wide. Fold in three, turn over, then place in the lightly greased tin.
4 Cover the dough with oiled clingfilm and leave to rise in a warm place for about 45 minutes, or until the dough has risen to the rim of the tin.
5 Brush with beaten egg, water or milk to glaze. Bake at 220° C (425° F) mark 7 for 20 minutes. Reduce the temperature to 180° C (350° F) mark 4 and remove the bread from the tin. Bake for a further 15 minutes. To test, tap the bottom crust; the bread should sound hollow. Cool on wire rack.

NOTE Dough made with fast-action dried yeast only requires one rising. Glazing with beaten egg produces a deep golden shiny finish; brushing with water gives a crisp crust; milk produces a soft, golden crust.

VARIATION *Soft White Bread:* Use strong white plain flour with 200 ml (7 fl oz) tepid milk and 75 ml (3 fl oz) tepid water.

MAYONNAISE

PREPARATION TIME 10-15 minutes
FREEZING Not suitable

MAKES 150 ML (5 FL OZ)
- *1 egg yolk*
- *2.5 ml (½ tsp) mustard powder or 5 ml (1 tsp) Dijon mustard*
- *2.5 ml (½ tsp) salt*
- *1.25 ml (¼ tsp) pepper*

140 CALS/15 ML (1 TBSP)
- *15 ml (1 tbsp) white wine vinegar or lemon juice*
- *about 150 ml (5 fl oz) oil*

1 Put the egg yolk in a bowl with the mustard, seasoning and 5 ml (1 tsp) of the vinegar or lemon juice. Mix thoroughly.

2 Add the oil drop by drop to begin with, then in a steady stream, whisking constantly, until the sauce is thick and smooth. If it becomes too thick, add a little more vinegar or lemon juice.

3 When all the oil has been added, add the remaining vinegar or lemon juice gradually and mix thoroughly. Store for up to 3 days in the refrigerator.

NOTE Never use eggs straight from the refrigerator as this may result in curdling.

PRESERVING TIPS

Making your own jams, jellies, chutneys and other preserves is one of the most satisfying ways of storing abundant seasonal fruit and vegetables. To achieve the best results, there are certain points about the process you should bear in mind.

PRESERVING EQUIPMENT

If you make a lot of preserves, it's worth investing in a proper preserving pan; the sloping sides help maintain a fast boil and reduce the chances of everything boiling over. Choose a pan made from stainless steel, tin-lined copper or lined aluminium. Don't use unlined aluminium.

If you don't have a preserving pan use a large heavy-based saucepan instead. Note that if you are using a saucepan rather than a preserving pan the preserve will take much longer to reach the setting point owing to the reduced surface area.

For jelly making, you will need a jelly bag for straining the juice from the cooked fruit. Although you can improvise with a large piece of muslin, a jelly bag is a worthwhile investment because it makes things easier. Whatever you use, it should be scalded with boiling water before use. If the jelly bag doesn't have a stand, suspend it from the legs of an upturned chair or stool.

TESTING FOR A SET

Jams, jellies, marmalades and conserves are cooked sufficiently when setting point is reached. There are various tests to determine this. Remove the pan from the heat while you are testing, to prevent overcooking.

Temperature test: The preserve is ready when the temperature registers 105°C (221°F) on a sugar thermometer.

Saucer test: Drop a spoonful of the preserve onto a chilled saucer and leave to cool. Push your finger through the jam; if the surface wrinkles, the preserve is ready.

Flake test: Using a wooden spoon, lift a little of the preserve out of the pan. Let it cool slightly then tip the spoon so that the preserve drops back into the pan; if the drips run together and fall from the spoon in a 'flake' rather than as drips, it is ready.

There is no accurate test for chutneys and pickles, because they are not cooked to a setting point. Instead, be guided by the consistency and cooking time specified in the recipe; they are ready when the mixture is very thick.

POTTING PRESERVES

All preserves should be potted into scrupulously clean containers. Wash jars or bottles in really hot soapy water, rinse thoroughly, then dry in a warm oven. Stand them upside down on a clean tea towel until the preserve is ready. Aim to pour hot jam or marmalade into the jars while they are still warm, to reduce the chances of the glass cracking, and fill them almost to the top. If potting jam, jelly, marmalade or conserve, cover with a waxed disc while the preserve is piping hot or else completely cold, then seal with a dampened clear disc secured with an elastic band. If you seal while the preserve is warm, mould will grow on the surface. Chutneys and pickles are covered in the same way. For long-term storage, cover the jar with a screw top as well.

FREEZING

Freezing is an easy and convenient way to preserve fresh food, allowing you to save and store for later use the wealth of seasonal delicacies that are available fresh for only a short time of the year. Whether you freeze ingredients in their basic state or made up into complete dishes, you will find a well-stocked freezer an invaluable help for producing nutritious meals with the minimum of fuss - especially if you also own a microwave for rapid thawing and reheating.

TIPS FOR EFFICIENT FREEZING

• Freeze only food of the best quality. Never freeze food that looks blemished or old.
• Handle the food as little as possible.
• Never put any foods that are still slightly warm into the freezer, as a rise in temperature causes frosting up and deterioration of other foods will result.
• Never freeze more than one tenth of your freezer's capacity in any 24 hours, as this will also cause the internal temperature to rise.
• When freezing large quantities, use the fast-freeze option.
• Pack and seal food with care. If moisture or cold air is allowed to come into contact with the food it will begin to deteriorate. Cross flavouring might also occur.
• Be sure to wrap non-packaged foods well before freezing. Solid foods must be packaged tightly, with as little air as possible. Wrap items in foil or freezer film; ordinary clingfilm is not suitable for the freezer. Freezer film can also be used as a lining for acidic foods which should then be over-wrapped in foil.
• Where possible use square containers to store food in the freezer; they stack better than round ones and therefore waste less space.
• Interleave any items of food that might otherwise stick together with pieces of greaseproof paper, polythene, foil or freezer film.
• When freezing liquids always leave room for expansion, as frozen liquid expands by about one-tenth of its volume and will push the lids off containers that have been overfilled.
• Freeze single and double portions for easy use.
• Keep you freezer as full as possible. If necessary add loaves of bread to fill up spaces. Empty spaces require more energy to keep cool.
• Make sure food is clearly labelled and dated.

Always use up old stocks first. To help you do this it is a good idea to keep a freezer log book, adding items (with the date) as you freeze them and deleting them as they are consumed.
• Do not re-freeze food once it has been thawed, unless it has been subsequently cooked.
• Check your freezer is operating correctly with a freezer thermometer. It should read -18°C (0°F).

FREEZER STORAGE CHART
This chart is a guide to approximate maximum storage times for certain types of food. Always follow the manufacturer's instructions.

VEGETABLES
blanched vegetables (most types) 10-12 months
mushrooms and tomatoes 6-8 months
vegetable purées 6-8 months

FRUIT
fruit in syrup 9-12 months
open frozen fruit 6-8 months
fruit purées 6-8 months
fruit juice 4-6 months

FISH
white fish 6-8 months
oily fish 3-4 months
fish portions 3-4 months
shellfish 2-3 months

MEAT AND POULTRY
beef and lamb 4-6 months
pork and veal 4-6 months
offal 3-4 months
sliced bacon/other cured meat 2-3 months
ham and bacon joints 3-4 months
chicken and turkey 4-6 months
duck and goose 4-6 months
venison 4-6 months
rabbit and game 4-6 months
sausages, sausagemeat 2-3 months
minced beef 3-4 months

PREPARED FOOD
soups and sauces 3 months
stock 6 months
prepared meals 4-6 months
  if highly seasoned 2-3 months
bread 2-3 months

pastries 3-4 months
cakes 4-6 months

DAIRY PRODUCE
cream 6-8 months
butter (salted) 3-4 months
cheese (hard) 4-6 months
cheese (soft) 3-4 months
ice cream, mousses etc 3-4 months

FREEZER EMERGENCIES

The most common freezer emergency is loss of power. This can be as a result of a power cut or someone inadvertently turning the freezer off. If there is a power cut, don't panic; if you leave the freezer door closed the food should stay frozen for about 30 hours (48 hours in a chest freezer). If possible, wrap the freezer with a blanket to increase insulation.

If you have advance warning of a power cut, turn on the fast-freeze switch, making sure the freezer is full to capacity. Towels or rolled newspaper can be used to fill any gaps.

Do not re-freeze any food you suspect may have begun to thaw.

FREEZING FRESH VEGETABLES

Vegetables can be very successfully frozen, but only if they are really fresh - no more than 12 hours after they were picked. Blanching the vegetables before freezing will help to preserve their colour, flavour and texture.

To blanch vegetables, bring a large pan of water to the boil and immerse the vegetables up to 450 g (1 lb) at a time. Bring back to the boil and keep the vegetables immersed for the required time - delicately textured or leafy vegetables such as spinach, mangetout and sliced courgettes will only need about 10 seconds, while firmer varieties such as broccoli and cauliflower florets, green beans and peas will need to be blanched for 1 minute. Root vegetables like carrots should be sliced and blanched for 2-3 minutes, while whole dense vegetables like globe artichokes and small beetroot need 4-5 minutes.

Once blanched, immediately remove the vegetables and plunge into a bowl of iced water. The blanching water can be used 6-7 times and the iced water refreshed with more ice as necessary. The vegetables can be put into a blanching basket for this part of the operation, but if you do not have one a suitable strainer or a large piece of muslin will do.

FREEZING FRESH FRUIT

First, check that the fruit you wish to freeze is properly ripe and in peak condition, free from any blemishes. Any overripe fruit should be puréed before freezing. With fruits such as apples you will have to cook them first before puréeing, but fruits such as peaches and raspberries can be puréed in their fresh form.

Before freezing the fruit, consider how it will eventually be used. Small fruits which do not need peeling are best frozen as they are; remove any stalks if necessary, and open freeze by spreading them on trays lined with non-stick paper, then transfer to polythene bags. They will not stick together, enabling small quantities to be removed as needed.

Firm fruits and any which have a tendency to discolour should be frozen in a syrup made with 450 g (1 lb) sugar to 1 litre (1¾ pints) water and the juice of 1 lemon. The fruits can be left whole, halved or sliced into the cool syrup as appropriate. For fruits such as grapefruit and pineapple omit the lemon juice and substitute any juice from the fruit.

THAWING FROZEN FOOD

Thawing must be done thoroughly and efficiently to ensure food is safe to eat.
• Never leave food to thaw in a warm environment; this is the ideal breeding ground for harmful bacteria. Instead, let the food thaw gradually in the refrigerator or in a cool larder.
• Cover food loosely while thawing.
• Make sure large items such as joints of meat are thoroughly thawed before cooking. The legs of poultry should be able to move freely.
• Dispose of any liquid which seeps from thawing meat and poultry. Do not allow it to come into contact with other food.
• Cook food as soon as possible after it is thawed.
• If thawing frozen food in a microwave, follow the manufacturer's instructions.
• Only use the microwave if you plan to eat or cook the food immediately.

INDEX